LEFT HAND IN THE GOLF SWING

... A Revised Look at Golf Cross-Training & Drills

by

R.D. HILL

Copyright 2012 by Robert Donovan Hill
All Rights Reserved

No part of this book may be reproduced, stored in a retrieval system, or transmitted in any form by any other means, electronic, mechanical, photocopying, recording or otherwise, without written permission from the author.

ISBN 10: 1479152129
ISBN 13:978 – 1479152124

Library of Congress Control Number: 2012949386

Printed in the United States of America
Donovan Hill Industries LLC, publisher

Front cover art by Steve Hardock
Rear cover photo by Steel Skye Photography

Contact the Author:

Email: rdhill@bellsouth.net

website: www.LeftHandintheGolfSwing.com

Any errors or omissions are entirely unintentional. If notified, the publisher will be pleased to make any necessary amendments at the earliest opportunity.

"The Buffalo Gnats
killed the mules,
the overflow
drowned the crops
and the malaria
rattled the teeth
of the family.

Yea,
though the oxen are slow,
the Earth is patient.

Endurance
hews a pathway to Truth.

Selah."

~ First Seven Lines are from a
University of Georgia
Alumni Solicitation,
... Circa 1964

Contents

Page

1.	Establishing the Left Hand Theory
7.	The Nature of Golf
8.	Shifting Your Viewpoint
9.	The Heart of the Matter
13.	Daily Activities Grow Talent, Too
15.	A Quick Check of Hand Strength
16.	Assessing Golf's Population
18.	Develop the Pulling Mechanics
20.	When the Golden Bear Spoke
23.	More on the Heart of the Matter
24.	Taking Stock
26.	Set a Schedule – Work a Plan
30.	Self-Test Your Ability
34.	Gauging Your Commitment
34.	Push vs Pull

37.	Visualization
38.	Why It Works
41.	More Drills
47.	Coming to Believe
50.	The Nature of Talent
51.	Golf's Talent – Spawned by Left-Hand Strength
55.	Fundamentals Need No Defense
56.	Dominant vs Subordinate Theory
59.	Patterned Training
62.	Cross-Training is Transference for Power & Control
67.	Stoking Your Passion
69.	Wisdom of a Hall-of-Famer
71.	Being Convinced
72.	Ted Williams on the Work Ethic
74.	Reference – Five Lessons: The Modern Fundamentals of Golf

81.	Handball – The Ambidextrous Sport
84.	Writing Lefty – A Worthy Endeavor
86.	What a Novelist Said About It
88.	Try Mirror Writing
90.	Work of the Thumb
93.	Speak to Your Muscles
95.	Know Thyself
97.	Facing Your Fear
103.	Develop Your Own Program
104.	Doing & Being: Work & Rest in the Learning Process
108.	Train Then Trust
109.	Pain as a Price for Progress
114.	Fluid Power has No Constraints
117.	The Incredible Efficiency of Unweighting
119.	Talent, Ability & Heart
121.	Re-Thinking Right Thinking

- **122.** Two-sided Cuts with a Baseball Bat
- **125.** The Fluid Hydraulics
- **127.** A Word of Caution
- **128.** The Subtleties of Strength & the Elements of Power
- **130.** Always Do Your Best
- **130.** Coming to Know the Athletic Golf Swing
- **133.** References
- **135.** About the Author

Establishing the Left Hand Theory

This is a How To book about improving your athletic and golfing ability.

It is an appeal to men and women who think it's too late to learn or improve to get serious with themselves and give it a go anyway. It exposes the *I'm too old* belief and the *I can't do it* charade.

The concepts and drills sneak up beside you and declare, 'Yes you can. SEE..?? You can't get there from HERE, but if you do this, FIRST, and master the task, you'll improve enough to do THIS, which will get you to HERE.' And you'll enjoy the endeavor.

MY HOPE IS TO INSPIRE YOUR PASSION FOR IMPROVEMENT

SPORTS LIKE GOLF – with complex physical mechanics – *seem* like mysteries to many who've missed the good instruction, or listened through ears of disbelief, because they weren't athletic superstars in their youth.

But careful readers will realize they don't *need* to have learned golf in childhood to become proficient and enjoy it as adults. They simply need to transfer their existing physical talents into the mechanics of the golf swing. This is a process, and it's what the book is about.

THE WRITING SEEKS TO SIMPLIFY GOLF – a game in which intricacy and difficulty *is* the draw, as well as the bane.

Golf is a physical game. Your Whole Body is the golf swing. Golf's great workout is *always* available to anyone who wants it. Improvement is acquired through diligent and guided practice, peppered with belief.

THE FOCUS IS ON TRUTHS fundamental to striking a golf ball. They are immutable nuggets gleaned through experience; highlighted and punctuated by wisdom from, among others: Ted Williams, Jack Nicklaus and Muhammad Ali.

* * *

YOUR GOLF SWING is a vital mix of universal fundamentals and personal idiosyncrasies blended by your style.

GOOD GOLF INSTRUCTION says many of the same things different ways, but little of it touts the beneficial balance of power acquired when the non-dominant hand's ability is brought on par with the dominant one. The left hand is the weaker for 90 percent of golfers.

THIS BOOK describes necessary and quantifiable benefits of the golf swing's pulling mechanics, and details similar techniques of other sports helpful to the golf swing. Tennis and the Frisbee toss are two favorites.

Applying the mechanics of sports that *complement* the action of the golf swing cross-trains talent into the swing.

THE BOOK is a formula for you to take stock of your golf game, set your own goals and be the sole judge of your progress. You're entitled and you are ABLE to grow your own talent. Don't let anyone tell you otherwise.

Your rate of improvement may be gradual or it might be sudden. Usually it varies task-to-task. Some things are easy; others you have to work at some. You won't know until you try.

Actual experience is the highest form of research. I encourage you to develop your own process of improvement, based on results *you feel in your swing and see in your game.* The book is chock full of suggestions and guidelines.

* * *

Golf is a two-handed game played sideways. There is synergy in the golf grip, with the leading upper hand pulling and the following lower one pushing, the clubhead.

Control and guide the club with the leading hand, and make the hit with the following one. That's the ideal.

SWING PROBLEMS OCCUR WHEN the dominant hand takes control of the club too early in the downswing – often with imperfect results. Therefore:

STRENGTHEN THE NON-DOMINANT HAND – THE HAND THAT *PULLS* – TO BALANCE THE POWER OF THE HANDS AS A UNIT, AND PLAY BETTER GOLF.

THUS THIS BOOK. But it's only a tool kit - A series of suggestions. Use what works and discard the rest. Tailor it to your own program. One I'll help you develop.

Lefty golfers please reverse things: Read right-for-left and left-for-right. The concepts are universal, but you can switch them in your head better than I can write around two points of view.

* * *

IMPROVING ATHLETICALLY IS NOT HARD. Simply intend to give your body enough time with the activities and drills to decide for yourself if your game is getting better, and if the investment is worth your while. You'll know in a week or ten days.

The physical rudiments to develop the left's latent physical prowess are described via the *pulling* mechanics of tennis and throwing a Frisbee left-handed – among other sports.

These sports and activities strengthen the left hand and arm and coordinate the torso's pivot process necessary to compress a golf ball.

For Righty golfers, playing Lefty tennis and Frisbee strengthens that arm through a similar and articulate range of motion *very similar* to the golf swing.

The Lefty tennis backhand brings a lot of swings into play very quickly. You don't need a ball or wall, yet. Just handle the racket in your left hand. Do air swings – hitting an imaginary volley. Stand before a mirror, if it helps.

Hand strength and coordination are called

upon immediately when you handle a tennis racket this way. Let your right hand teach your left, if you play better Righty. This is a simple and inexpensive way to improve your golf swing. And it's Fun! – Fun because it is so simple, practical and beneficial.

AND *NEVER* DISCOUNT the hand strength and dexterity attained through activities like playing guitar or piano, for examples. Or hand waxing your car using only your left, or washing windows with it.

Walk a strong dog with the leash in your non-dominant hand to get a feel for the strength you'll need. You get the picture.

THE BENEFITS of these and other sports and activities are examined in detail. There's no guesswork. It's a formula laid out in action-packed detail.

THE FORMULA is that you develop and practice a process to bring your talent into play by cross-training what you know from other sports and activities to play better golf.

You won't have to overhaul your golf swing. You're going to bring new talent to it – strength and control – and have fun doing it. You'll play better golf, shoot lower scores and have more fun out there.

The Nature of Golf

Life may imitate art, but sport is more apt to call forth the living of it. No game more than golf tests human nature - attributes we esteem in others and seek to enhance in ourselves.

Golf is a hard game. All who play, struggle with it. The ardent golfer is always working the kinks out of something.

Nature established *struggle* to ensure the full development of potential. By design, striving is the perfect motivator toward elusive excellence.

Sports played well hone skills that oil the moves in the game of life. Talent blends with opportunity and analysis to present a chance that demands a decision. An action is taken. Ground is gained. A goal is closer, or reached. Good golf plays like that.

Life's choices are often irreversible and of great consequence. We discern through ideals like risk and reward, letting go to gain and self-discipline and the work ethic.

The golfer's road to improvement is an avenue of self-discovery. Because it's a *Game of Good Misses*, the committed golfer faces human imperfection with every stroke. One looks in the mirror every time s/he stands over a golf ball – club in hand – To execute a shot.

Nobody hits it flush every time. All golfers will hit the errant shot, and face the consequence. Pros and Amateurs alike know the feelings of abject failure from chili-dipping a simple chip shot, or stubbing a wedge.

Most players agree water more than sand alters the nature of their swing, but distance, too, can take one out of one's game. Sometimes nothing seems longer than a two-foot breaking putt. Downhill.

Because golf inspires as often as it instructs, your best shots invariably follow your worst. That's golf's allure.

Perhaps Arnold Palmer – The King - Described The Greatest Game best:

"Golf is deceptively simple and endlessly complicated.... it satisfies the soul and frustrates the intellect....it is at the same time rewarding and maddening – and it is without a doubt the greatest game mankind has ever invented."

Shifting Your Viewpoint

STRIKE A MATCH in a dark room and it will change your outlook. Simply *make a beginning* and your perspective will change enough to decide if progress is worth your commitment of time and effort.

Get ready to leave your present platform of ability for a new one. Benchmark your improvement by how you play a certain nemesis hole on your home course

You may find yourself going for a green from distance instead of laying up behind a water hazard, or driving a series of traps you used to regularly play out of.

NEW THINGS take time and repetition, so I'll repeat myself, or say the same things different ways more than once. Consider it practice for your hearing, much like hitting a bucket of balls is practice for your golf swing.

The Heart of the Matter

TO BE PROFICIENT at golf, certain natural physical tendencies must be overcome by a prescribed athletic manifestation, trained into being - Not thought about when executed, but practiced into the physical subconscious. Some call it muscle memory.

It is actually *Tissue Intelligence*. Science has proven muscles have intelligence at the cellular level.

The psycho-biology of the Somatic

Practices – a developing knowledge of how the body learns - Asserts that new skills can become *more than good ideas.* They become naturally developing actions and habits one cares about and moves toward in competency.

Desire spawns success. Then success reinforces success, and you're on your way. This is the substance of *Left Hand in the Golf Swing* - exploring the mind/body relationship of physical learning.

Muscle memory's place is to do exactly what intelligent muscle tissue tells it to do. Let's take that muscle tissue to school..!!

* * *

Golf is a full physical commitment. Pro athletes agree it's one of the hardest athletic maneuvers to master. Your whole body is the golf swing. It's a great workout, and because it's a game played sideways, other sports played to the side have natural physical attributes that mirror and enhance the golf swing, from the bottom of the feet to the gripped fingers of the hands set high in the backswing.

DRILLS ARE GOLF PRACTICE. This book describes a host of activities you can turn into drills for your golf swing – Things you can do daily to improve instead of just hitting buckets of balls by rote. Save your money, use time wisely and get better. That's win/win.

CONSIDER TENNIS, and picture the tennis racket raised across the body hitting the high backhand volley. That's one of the toughest shots in tennis, yet it is *very similar in technique to the golf swing* – As stated. So is the Lefty tennis backhand - Very similar mechanics to golf.

THE HIGH-BACKHAND VOLLEY – ONE OF THE TOUGHEST SHOTS IN TENNIS - IS THE TYPICAL GOLF SWING.

Doesn't it follow, then: Improve your Lefty tennis to improve your golf?

NOW CONSIDER THE FRISBEE. As you prepare to toss a Frisbee left handed, you waggle it loosely in your fingers. Then you bring the Frisbee clear up past your right ear as you torque and turn your body in preparation to release it.

Then you release your hips and torso with your head still – perhaps even moving the head backward a fraction as you release - Your hand and fingers are laid open as you extend your arm to impart the last iota of control to the spinning disc, to get it on line – On target.

Oh yeah, cross-training with a Frisbee will enhance your golfing ability..!!

LEFTY TENNIS IS A SIMPLE DRILL, BUT NOBODY SAID IT IS EASY

Nobody said golf is easy, either. It's not. *Golf is hard and it's hard to get good at.* But 34 percent of golfers pursue a handicap or track their scoring averages because they *want* to improve. If you're in that group or want to be, then welcome aboard.

CONSIDER: If you're a natural at baseball, then you can throw a curve ball. You don't; your muscles do. All you do is look at a target, throw and release. Your mind has the intent and your muscles have the intelligence to get the job done. They've been trained through practice.

SAME WITH dribbling a basketball with either hand, or passing behind your back.

You weren't born with the ability, but at some point in your basketball life, you decided to improve your ball-handling skills, liked how it felt and practiced until you had the confidence to use new ability in a game – Like the behind-the-back pass.

Might've been your senior year of varsity basketball, but you *owned it* by then, and the skill made you a better player.

You could deliver the ball running full speed with touch, or bounce it with spin, behind your back.

YOUR BODY'S MUSCLE TISSUE regarding that skillful endeavor was made smarter because you paid attention to the certain idiosyncrasies it took to execute a particular pass with intent, delivered via synergy contributed by your fingers, wrist, arm and shoulders.

Those muscles have *intelligence*, because they can adjust to what it takes to deliver the ball *just the way you want it and at a moment's notice.* Fast. Slow. At a trot or running wide open. Now see yourself owning the same ability with a golf club. You *can*.

Daily Activities Grow Talent, Too

Don't be concerned if you don't play tennis or hockey or swing a baseball bat.

Switching hands to do your everyday tasks and chores will build talent in your developing left hand, as well. You simply have to use it to do your daily tasks – Whether it's pulling clothes from the dryer or scrubbing a frying pan clean.

The Karate Kid's *Wax on - Wax off* mantra has merit if you work both hands in both directions. You go to your dominant hand now mostly out of habit.

EATING WITH YOUR OFF HAND, or

scrambling eggs, or brushing your teeth or buttoning a button with the unaccustomed appendage – These activities bring touch and talent to your non-dominant hand and fingers.

That bettered ability transfers to your handling a golf club. Try it. Commit to the effort 10 minutes a day every-other-day for a week. If you don't gain dexterity, you'll probably find you need to.

Every-other-day is only four days of the week. Ten minutes of effort is all you need to get it started. Ten *attempts* is sufficient for the drills and activities you find real difficult.

EXPECT THE GOLF CLUB to feel differently in your hands as you progress.

You're succinctly more capable. Confident. Putts and chips present themselves with new options. Your grip is delivering more feedback via new muscle intelligence in your hands and fingers, giving your mind more shot choices.

You just feel better over the ball. Your ball strikes are cleaner, and your scores reflect that.

IT TAKES the hands of a surgeon to do some of golf's best work - To feather a chip or caress a putt. You *can develop* that kind of touch. Why? Because:

AS THE LEFT IMPROVES, SO DOES THE GOLF GAME

Test this thinking. Determine its value, and use what works for you.

A Quick Check of Hand Strength

Grab a couple of broadsheets of newspaper. Get two pieces – one for each hand. Use a double-wide section. Start at a corner and wad up a sheet in the palm of each hand, with the hands working freely from one another.

Do this standing up. You can twist and contort each arm around as you work your fingers and thumbs, but don't assist one hand with the other and don't anchor your forearms or elbows to your torso or thighs.

Flex your hands freely from perpendicular, or raise them in front of you, or angle your forearms upward. Whatever aids your struggle? Just scrunch your fingers and draw the paper up into your palms, wadding the sheets into tight balls, each hand doing its own labor.

How's that feel? Probably your fingers are stiff and your forearms are burning. Perhaps one more than the other. You may have had to rest and start again. That's okay.

VARY YOUR METHOD and do it with your forearms resting on a table in front of you. This takes your arms and shoulders out of it and puts all the work on the fingers.

Strengthening the fingers can be a lengthy process (weeks, not months), because there's not a lot of bulk muscle in them. They're slender. You'd have no dexterity if they weren't.

If you'll crumple a couple of sheets of newspaper every-other-day, you'll develop strong, nimble fingers in hands that control the golf club with a lot more authority than you've ever had.

Prove it to yourself - And swing your golf clubs after working any drill, even if you're just nipping dollar weed out of your lawn. It reminds your golf muscles of your intent.

Assessing Golf's Population

Righty Golfers play from the left side of the ball when looking through the green. Golf's a two-handed game played sideways- Most often played by right-hand-dominant athletes.

Statistics reveal about 90 percent of golfers swing a golf club right handed; so they grip the club with the dominant right hand placed below the left on the grip.

The non-dominant left leads, and *pulls* the clubhead through the arc of the swing. The right hand trails the left, and *pushes* the clubhead.

Ideally, the hands work as a unit, with the left guiding and controlling, and the right contributing its power only at the bottom of the swing.

But too often – because it *can* - the dominant right hand takes control too early in the down swing. An off-line swing and poor ball contact is the most likely result. Fades, and pulls and miss-hits are in that mix.

THE WEAKER LEFT HAND and arm that leads the golf swing of the Righty golfer provides an uncertain pivot point through which the wrists break.

A strong and coordinated left arm will control the club through the desired swing plane on-line, and augments the pivot of the wrist break with repetitious certainty. The right applies power at the bottom of the swing.

Strengthen the left appendage to offset the dominant right's over-influence in the swing. You'll handle the club better. Development is essential to the two-handed balance consistent ball striking best responds to.

A BALANCE OF POWER IS WHAT'S REALLY BEING DISCUSSED HERE

The dominant right hand is mollified (appeased, tempered) by the controlled pull the left hand contributes to keeping the club on-line.

Now you're enjoying golf with the two-handed balance-of-power that creates better ball striking and lower scores. You'll have more fun out there. Plan to play more than practice, in your future.

Develop the Pulling Mechanics

Enhanced left-hand ability will *naturally bring talent* to your game by creating new athletic choices within the swing.

The proof is in your improvement – Cloaked as talent. Once you come to believe you can get better, you'll live your own road to growth in golf. You'll work the formula – Your Process - And if you're in it for the long haul, you'll experience steady improvement and enjoyment in the game.

Expect to feel better over the ball - More confident of your ability to hit different shots, as your shot choices expand.

GOLF IS A GREAT WAY TO BE OUTSIDE. It's quality family time and great alone time, too. Why not enhance the experience with the soul-satisfying pleasure gained from striking the ball well? Why not enjoy golf *'till you can't get enough of it?*

I believe we as individuals are divinely wired to play games – sports – and there's a lot of choice in how you spend your free time. Make golf fun and you'll find more time for it.

CONSIDER: It is more profitable to strengthen the weak left hand than weaken the dominant right. *How can two weak hands keep a club on plane and precisely strike the back of the ball?*

THE FOLLOWING ACTION-PACKED PAGES are chock full of examples, exercises and advice proven to coordinate and strengthen your off-side torso, shoulder, arm and hand to enable you to hit a golf ball with trusted repetition.

Once your body embraces the learning, expect your creative imagination to go beyond what's introduced – To the subtle nuance of left hand / right hand dominance in *your own* hobbies, and the work you do.

IF YOU'RE INTRIGUED then you're on your way. It IS a process, not an event. Left hand ability comes at a different pace for different people. Some aspects of dexterity are gained quickly; others, slowly.

SOMETIMES YOU HAVE TO OWN ALL of a thing to have any of its benefits, so work hard. Persevere. Pay attention to how you feel about how you're hitting it. Practice with a favorite club.

The key is to begin and persist, yet never quit playing golf. Keep swinging your clubs as you cross-train and drill to remind your muscle tissue why you're training it.

When the Golden Bear Spoke

Striking a golf ball is an act of violence performed under the auspices of grace and goodwill. It is an unparalleled athletic endeavor that ranks professional golfers among the best athletes.

JACK NICKLAUS – THE ACKNOWLEDGED GREATEST GOLFER OF ALL TIME - was Sport's Illustrated Athlete of the Decade in the 1970's, and was recognized by ESPN as the Individual Athlete of the Century in the year 2000. Michael Jordan was voted Team Athlete of the Century.

I've heard no arguments against either award, but I've heard non-golfers (and non-athletes) describe golf as an activity, and compare it to billiards or archery.

Tell a bow hunter he's not an athlete, but be careful. I'm one of the worst bowlers I know, but I will *always appreciate* how Pros in that sport send the ball down the lane.

Nearly seven out of ten professional and world-class amateur athletes pursue golf as a hobby. Men and women. Why? Because golf is hard, and great athletes are challenged by it. It's that simple.

Though most Professional football and baseball players retire at an age young enough to compete in golf at the professional level, few make the transition. Why? Because ability in the game demands a maturation period.

Pro athletes who golf recreationally rarely develop the skill necessary to compete on the PGA Tour or other professional golf tours. Devotion to their own sport doesn't afford time necessary to be Pros at both.

ACTIVITY OR SPORT...?? NO CONTEST...!!

THE JACK NICKLAUS ARTICLE published in Tennis Magazine in the mid-1970's affirmed beliefs about golf I had entertained since my first hacking swing with a long iron as a child.

When he's dialing it in, Nicklaus wears one of the most malevolent game faces in sport.

Though his talent usually lies within a calm demeanor, it is delivered under pressure through eyes discerning as a linebacker's.

In the mid-1970's, Jack Nicklaus was pictured on Tennis Magazine's front cover, serving up a tennis ball to lady Pro Kathy Rinaldi on a grass court in his back yard in North Palm Beach.

Jack is right handed, and said in the subsequent interview that he played Righty to compete with Rinaldi, but admitted that in deference to his golf swing, he should be playing left-handed.

CONSIDER: THE GREAT ONE – The *'Best Who Ever Did It'* in golf – said playing tennis left-handed would benefit his golf swing. If it matters to Jack, what should it mean to you and me?

At the very *least*, I reasoned, if some is good, then more is better, so why not REALLY climb on board?

WHY NOT ESTABLISH A DOMINANT LEFT HAND?

Now Jack is probably a pretty even-handed athlete. He was an All-Ohio honorable mention guard in basketball his senior year of high school, recruited by Ohio State and other universities.

Typically, a Professional athlete more

naturally develops both sides of the body, so a Pro athlete's off hand in any sport is better than the Amateur's, but Mr. Nicklaus did not make his statement as a casual reference or off-hand remark (pun unintentional). His thoughts resonated truth to me.

Jack Nicklaus had spoken and I had heard. So I set out to improve my left.

More on the Heart of the Matter

How many swing faults are rooted in inability? Well that IS the game, isn't it?

Golf is about ability, or getting around 18 holes without it. The golf swing is limited by what one can do athletically with the club in hand.

NOT EVERYONE can hit all the shots with all the clubs, but golfers who hit the broadest range of shots shoot the lower average scores. Hence, *golfers score by learning to manage their swing faults*.

We all ride plateaus of ability in this game, then work around certain shortcomings over time and go forward - if we're lucky. And persistent.

SOME SWING FAULTS BECOME INGRAINED GOLFING PROBLEMS

For example: Poor coaching will allow a weak non-dominant left hand to lock out into the hammer grip of the baseball swing - Which gives the golfer a feeling of strength - But it's a fraud that produces a fade or a deep slice.

A ball sliced is usually struck well, and the typical golfer likes the feel of the hit, but has no idea how to straighten it out. Close the stance, strengthen the grip...??

These short-term swing fixes are extremes which often create other lasting problems.

Compensating poor swing mechanics by adjusting the stance or a weird grip adjustment often brings a golfer to the point of critically analyzing the relevance of the sport in their recreational lives. Take heart, if this is you. There is a solution.

Taking Stock

DEVELOPING AN ATHLETIC GOLF SWING is a Process, not an Event.

Get quiet somewhere and assess how you feel about your ability and what you want out of golf.

If you can get there with what you've got, then you should already be there in mind, will and temperament.

You exude the success of it, and – that

attained – You're going after your next victory or next par or next challenge in life with the unspoken certainty it takes to succeed.

IF, ON THE OTHER HAND, you've got work to do, then you've got work to do.

* * *

Ambition is a curse *and* a blessing, but there is nothing so honest as desire. If you have that, then get yourself working a program of improvement, and determine to enjoy the journey.

The measure of effort over time may be documented, but the commitment is understood only by those who undergo the experience.

BE TOUGH ON YOURSELF, BUT BE PATIENT, TOO

If you believe *nothing* is acceptable if it can be improved, then you're on your way to a level of excellence in golf and sport that will enhance your sense of well-being in any endeavor, and every encounter life gives you.

IN A TELEVISION INTERVIEW, the actor Richard Dreyfus commented on his work in a film done early in his career. "I didn't like it," he said. "I could see me trying."

Get used to it. Get used to trying. Pro

athletes put heart and soul on the line every day they practice or compete. It's nice to hit it smooth with a smile, but life isn't that way when you're learning something new.

IT TAKES GUTS to grind it out and teach muscles new ways to work.

It takes grit to play golf, and a plateful to play it with a smile. But you've probably already decided it's worth it.

If you have passion for golf, you think of it much; but golf is a game that has to be played.

Enjoying your round is what it's all about, isn't it? It's fun to reminisce, too, the good shots, but you've got to bring home the score to really relish them. Nobody savors a bad finish. Hitting the ball well livens the color of your memories.

IF THE DESIRE IS IN YOU, golf will bring you time and again to a place that demands your excellence and establish you with a soul-satisfied keener sense of it - Either acute knowledge of your strengths or a humbling awareness of your shortcomings. Any good round of golf usually delivers a blend.

Set a Schedule – Work a Plan

10 minutes a day every other day in a drill is only four days a week, yet it's much more

effective practice than spending an hour on Saturday doing the same thing. Why?

Because muscles asked to learn something carry new fresh memory of the benefits into subsequent sessions.

Why make your golf swing wait all week? Muscles forget, just as minds do.

You're not too old or unskilled to learn. You can gain athletic prowess at any age.

Nautilus training is proved to benefit all who work the machines. What are golf drills but a variation of something proven beneficial?

THERE IS SOMETHING worthy deposited in the hearts of all competitive men and women – and boys and girls - that derives satisfaction from the grind and discipline it takes to learn, improve and excel at an intricate physical discipline.

Yoga, gymnastics, dance, judo, karate – they all qualify. Dojos and gyms are filled with committed enthusiasts. Golf fits right into this equation.

Sports pundits say golf demands the keenest sense of awareness mankind can derive from a game. If you do any of the above, you can golf.

Self-discipline parents your priorities. When drilling, think of playing *with it* instead of working *at it.* You're simply paying attention to a few things.

The intent is to improve your pleasure in the game. Golf and life are meant to be enjoyed. Golf gives back through the pleasure of good shot making.

* * *

SOME SAY HITTING A BASEBALL is harder than hitting a golf ball, because it's a round bat striking a round ball travelling over 90 mph vs the golfer hitting the stationary smaller ball with the flat face of a golf club, swinging at his or her own tempo, when ready.

Hey, neither is easy, and there aren't droves of major leaguers retiring from baseball in their mid-30's to hit the PGA Tour in what would be their athletic primes, are there? They are similar – but separate – athletic disciplines.

IF YOU'RE ONBOARD, then get yourself on a schedule.

Remember: 10 minutes a day every other day is better than an hour on a weekend. If you miss a few days, don't worry about it. Just catch the next train and get back on a schedule.

Quit early sometimes or skip a couple days and see if it makes you eager to get back to it. Make your practice fun and stay hungry.

PREPARE TO BUILD talent and ability

into your body to take your game to a higher level.

The ideal state is to be satisfied with your status, while embracing your potential. You are the sole judge of that standard.

Improving at golf takes diligence – a steady effort over time - But the rudiments of practice are a labor of love for most golfers.

SOME OF GOLF INSTRUCTION can be criticized for failing to share with the golfing public that golf is hard and it's hard to get good at it. That's a simple truth.

We live in a society where Fun, Fast & Easy supplants diligence, and trophies and ribbons are awarded for showing up. That's not life, and it's not golf.

On the other hand, I'm encouraged to see many young skateboard enthusiasts honing their skills with diligence – Practicing day after day after day. Passion hasn't gone out of style. The world is full of committed young people chasing their dreams.

If you're still reading, then you have a cultivated interest in the game of golf – perhaps a passion for it - And you're seeking a method of improvement.

GOLF HAS EMBRACED YOU BECAUSE YOU HAVE EMBRACED IT

You find the give-and-take worthwhile. It pays to know what to practice. Let's get started.

Self-Test Your Ability

Opportunities to strengthen your weaker hand abound.

Hold a phone book, dictionary or Bible in your dominant hand. Get a heavy one. Now put the book in your off hand and open it to the middle. Move it to the strong hand. Feel better? Of course it does! Now move it over to your weak hand. Snap it shut, then relax your hand and allow the book to open. Feel weird?

Odds are good your forearm is burning, or perhaps your ring finger and pinkie; or your thumb may be numb. Vary the weight distribution by looking up different words.

Raise and lower the book to different heights and angles. Switch hands, and gauge your weak hand against the dominant one. Let your strong hand teach the weaker one. You're seeking a balance of power here.

No pain, no gain speaks directly to what you're accomplishing. Grit your teeth and endure the burn when it comes. Just keep your goals in sight. A little effort every day is better than a lot all at once.

NOW PICK UP A PEN with your off hand.

Underline a word in the dictionary. Can you make a clean, precise line? Do it with the dominant hand, then use the weaker one. Compare the difference.

Ink in the hollow cavity of an O or D. Stay within the lines. Be quick and efficient with the pen. This may tire your arm up to the shoulder.

Let your strong hand handle the pen and show you how it *should* feel, then work toward that feeling using the other hand. This is an acid test of the strength and subtle dexterity you're gaining command of.

CHECK THE HANDLE of a locked door with an extended left hand. Turn the doorknob left and right, and then shake the door. Feel the strength coursing up through your shoulder? It wells up from the sole of your anchored left foot, if your left hand is on the doorknob.

TURN A KEY in a deadbolt with the left thumb and forefinger. Lock it and unlock it several times. How's that feel? It might be difficult to your untrained hand. The thumb may let you down. What if the lock won't budge? What if you can't do it?

HERE'S A TRUTH: **'*I can't get there from here*'** really does apply sometimes.

Sometimes you've got to build strength in an easier activity to do a more difficult thing later. But you always come back to it with better ability.

ROTATE A BALLED-UP FIST. Tire it in one direction, and then reverse it. This is great for the forearms and wrists.

In the developing Left, the rotational ability will be limited initially in and around the wrist bone, but rotate it regularly and the wrist will form a marvelous working alliance with the hand, just as your dominant hand has done. Use your strong hand as a model.

UNZIP A ZIPPER gripping the zipper tang with your weaker thumb and forefinger, or work the zip lock tab on a bag of dog food back-and-forth a few times.

Strength comes from the shoulder, and it takes *real strength and coordination* to be fast and fluid here.

USE YOUR DOMINANT HAND to model the action for the weaker one. Remember how it feels done easily, and bring that memory immediately to the off hand, then execute.

Note the difference in clarity in memory and feel with each hand. You can only recall as vividly as you can actually DO an activity - But practicing the recall will have you doing it better the next time you attempt it physically.

EVOKING MEMORY IMPROVES THE PHYSICAL. PRACTICE IMBEDS A BETTER MEMORY. ONE WILL ALWAYS ENHANCE THE OTHER. TRUE - EVEN IF YOU'RE INEPT AT THE OUTSET

HOLD YOUR CELL PHONE in your left hand against your right ear with the palm facing away from your face. The thumb and forefinger grip the phone. This can be a tough little isometric exercise.

ABILITY in these subtle endeavors takes *real strength*. Expect strength and even-handed coordination to develop quickly. Maintain that positive expectation.

Consciously use the weaker hand in an activity. It doesn't have to be difficult. But you do have to choose to use it. Make it a habit.

No need to grit and grimace. Just do it. You're bringing a minor physical shortcoming into your awareness without judgment or ridicule. *You're simply paying attention to it with an expectation of change.*

Strength creates *feel,* and allows for an unhurried pace, or any pace you want.

The touch you'll develop by writing left handed – for example - will correlate to the subtle control of the clubhead, especially on delicate chips around the green; and when putting.

Gauging Your Commitment

Not all exercises are easy at the out-set. Try the toughest drills some, even if they seem impossible.

The mental angst can be tough as the physical, but paying attention to a drill or exercise a little every day builds strength and coordination. Over time, elusive talent will arrive. Sometimes you've got to get all of a thing to own any of it.

Trust your awareness, and expect more feel in the physical set-point positions.

You'll feel more confident taking your stance over the ball, in the backswing, at the set position or making the hit. Celebrate that... You're on your way...!!

Push vs Pull

The act of pulling the arm backhand across the body is a more consistent and powerful motion than pushing it – once learned - But it's not natural unless you grew up flinging a Frisbee or playing tennis Lefty.

There aren't many other common sports / activities that mimic the independent left-hand pulling motion golf expects.

Fencing, and cracking a whip sideways, and karate's backhand strike are about all that come to mind.

Rotating the counter-clockwise end of a long jump rope would strengthen the left, but odds are good you used your dominant right as a child, because it was the more coordinated hand and the stronger arm.

That's the thing: We've used the stronger arm because it worked better, making a task easier. Using it became habit.

* * *

WHEN PULLING across the body with either arm, the muscles of the torso pivot, providing leverage and support. If you've little strength in your left and you golf Righty, you're golfing with a dominant right side delivering power through the right hand at the bottom of the swing.

A pulling action in the left to balance that strong right is the reason for new strength.

STRENGTHEN THE PULLING ARM TO ADD CONTROL TO POWER & CONSISTENCY TO YOUR BALL STRIKING

CONSIDER: A CARD TOSSED DEFTLY onto a poker table is sent spinning with a backhand motion. The backhand strike is banned in boxing, because of its power. Karate's spinning back kick delivers a phenomenally powerful blow, as well.

Tennis great Don Budge had a backhand that was his bread-and-butter shot - The one he could rely on to win a point outright when he needed it. They said Budge hit a *heavy* ball - One that had deceptive pace on it. True, because he knew how to get *behind* the ball.

CONSIDER these non-athletic pulling motions: I *pull* my garbage bin to the curb once a week, and would rather *pull* my luggage through an airport, than push it. My Christmas storage bins behave better when I pull them across the floor from storage.

MANAGERS IN LEADERSHIP say you can't push a rope or chain. You've got to pull it. Leaders lead. Good leaders pull, they don't push.

A clubhead follows better when led – (pulled, controlled) – by a strong arm. The trailing hand adds the balance of power to the ball strike at the bottom of the swing.

WATCH SWING FLAWS FALL to the wayside as you strengthen your non-dominant hand.

True, there's effort to it, but you'll find it beats the heck out of spraying a bucket of balls all over the driving range, then driving home wondering why you even bothered going there in the first place.

* * *

Consider the competitive swimmer. S/he trains several days, clocks a time with the coach for a benchmark, then resumes training.

Shooting a score or hitting a bucket is benchmarking your talent, and talent's progress. But *practice builds ability. Drills are the optimum practice.*

Test this for yourself. Make a decision to commit for a time, and then gauge your progress.

Visualization

VISUALIZATION plays a big part in training a physically immature body.

Former PGA Tour Pro and golf commentator Curtis Strange has said it's one of the biggest parts of the game. It has much to do with sewing the seeds of talent harvested later in better ability.

MENTAL FAMILIARITY CAN BE TANGIBLE

Feel a lemon slice between your teeth.

Now bite down. This one's easy. It's the difficult physical mechanics that are hard to visualize. You're not alone. It takes practice to make them tangible as lemon juice.

Thinking through what we know imbeds it freshly in our minds, and the next athletic session is bolstered by the accurate memory of that most recent best effort.

Regular and honest self-assessment determines an acceptable course of future improvement. The view of the landscape changes with each session of effort, as does the work required to grow the talent.

Why It Works

GOOD GOLF INSTRUCTION says many of the same things different ways, but little of it advocates the necessity for left hand dominance, or ambidextrous talent.

You've come this far. Give your body enough time with the drills to decide for yourself if you're getting better.

Be the sole judge of your standards. Set your own goals. Think of ways to improve your off hand in your work or everyday life.

Make a list, Work a plan and Trust your creative self to have you doing what will benefit you most.

HITTING GOLF BALLS BY ROTE IS NOT THE ANSWER

Hitting a bucket is a great gauge of progress, but not the prime developer of ability. Those who've peaked and shelved their clubs can tell you about it.

WHY NOT CROSS-TRAIN with a sport or activity? Focus on strength in your weaker hand and develop the rhythmic tension, flow and follow through good golf demands.

This is play, not work, but it's OK to work at play. It's a positive obsession. A healthy escape; and when you DO hit balls, note how you're hitting them better. Meanwhile, learn tennis or hockey or fencing, or ping-pong. Or guitar – Using your left to improve your golf.

A CASE CAN BE MADE that a Make-It-Fun or Quick-Fix mentality is the best way to introduce golf to adults and children.

Too much early harsh reality in a difficult endeavor turns off some of the would-be enthusiasts, some say.

Feed the newcomers the difficult stuff in small doses and they'll remain intrigued and reap golf's benefits down life's road.

Perhaps, but ignoring the need for certain strengths does newcomers a disservice.

SMART CROSS-TRAINING SIMPLIFIES THE LEARNING

Too much of golf instruction ignores the two-handed balance necessary for success. Never Mentions It.

Breaking down the athletic mechanics to simpler form via other similar sports makes golf interesting and fun. It's better to build a swing from there. Some *really bad habits* can get ingrained unless you're focusing on the fundamentals.

EXAMPLE: Once a beginner is hitting it *wristy* but making good contact - it can be real hard to EVER get them turning the torso and driving through with the legs.

CONSIDER: It is so simple – and practical, and beneficial – to get a group of golf students out of the rain and under the cart barn throwing Frisbees left-handed than to just cancel a lesson due to wet weather.

Disc Golf is all about pulling an arm across the body with intent - Delivering an object accurately. Traditional golf teaching ignores a primary fundamental setting this aside.

USEFUL GOLF INSTRUCTION sidles up alongside and enables your athletic mind to see itself differently within the problem. And it offers a solution: *It is the solution.*

Knowledge makes you your own best coach, and ability made natural stays with you. But you've got to think outside the box to handle the club in new ways. Hence, these suggestions and rationale.

More Drills

Tennis, Frisbee and racquetball are great for cross-training, but there are many useful sports and activities that profit the left hand. Here's a few more:

SWING A BAT to build wrist strength. It's a good training aid if you know what your hands are doing. More later on this.

DRIVE with only your weaker hand on the steering wheel. Drive sharp curves that way. See how the shoulder gets involved? You're making critical and beneficial demands on dormant muscle groups.

Grip the steering wheel tightly for several seconds; now relax it. Do it palms up and palms down on various parts of the wheel. Note which angles tire you quickest, and do them first next time.

YOU MAY HAVE SOME PAIN in your left hand from squeezing the wheel. Cartilage and muscles are working new ways. Vary the pressure among the fingers.

Rhythmically drum your fingers on your car's rooftop. Drive each fingertip into the

LEFT HAND IN THE GOLF SWING

roof separately, and hold it. Bring the thumb into play. Work out various syncopations.

TO IMPROVE QUICKLY, work on what's difficult. Most likely your pinkie and ring finger will feel weakest or tire first. These fingers control the butt of the club. Improve them, and improve your golf. But don't ignore the thumb.

CONSIDER: The thumb is the only appendage truly *behind* the shaft of your leading hand, in a strong grip. That's the Left hand for Rightys, right hand for Lefty's. More later on this, too.

LEAN YOUR WEAK-SIDE SHOULDER against a wall or doorjamb with your arm extended down by your side. Extend your fingers and *push out* with the back of your hand, moving your shoulders and torso off the wall. Locate the stress points. Probably in the top of your forearm or shoulder.

Relax your hand and do it again. Fall back into the door jamb slowly. You're coordinating power. Slow your fall with the back of the fingers hitting first, then the wrist and rest of the arm, working from low-to-high.

FOR MORE PULLING RESISTANCE, extend your left arm straight out in front of you, connecting the back of the hand against a doorjamb, wall or pole – anything to provide resistance – And push against it. This will torque you clockwise. Now pivot back into it. Work this at various angles, including your golf setup position.

HANG BY ONE HAND, THEN THE OTHER from a chin-up bar. Grab a bar you don't have to jump to reach. Just let your legs go and hang until the bar is pulled through your fingers.

Usually, the bicep reveals a lack of development, and the grip weakens. It's an acid test of true strength, and a great strength developer.

BRUSH YOUR TEETH left-handed without bloodying your gums, and apply toothpaste, too. Screw the cap back on with the unnatural hand. Reverse everything. Let the dominant hand teach the weak one.

APPLY AFTERSHAVE, soap a washcloth or use your back brush with the unaccustomed hand. Open a child-proof prescription bottle with your off hand. It is harder than it looks.

SWITCH HANDS washing dishes. Peel an onion, slice tomatoes or butter your bread with your off hand. Safely using a sharp knife is another acid test of manipulative ability. Pull the laundry from the washer with your off hand. Load the dryer the same way.

LEFT HAND IN THE GOLF SWING

TEAR A PIECE OF PAPER from a legal pad with your off hand, or rip a check from your check book. It takes power and finesse from deep within the bone – Core strength. Another acid test of off-hand dexterity.

TOTE YOUR SCHOOL BOOKS beneath your weaker arm, or loop your book bag over the non-dominant shoulder.

IT TAKES ABILITY in a variety of activities to bring forth talent and touch. Address and practice various lefty drills one-by-one. They are all unique undertakings.

LIKE THE WORDS OF A LANGUAGE, THE MORE ACTIVITIES YOU MASTER, THE MORE YOUR TALENT WILL INCREASE

AS STRENGTH DEVELOPS in your non-dominant hand, you'll become aware of how much you *put your shoulder* into the physical things you do.

You do it unconsciously on your strong side. Even the intricate stuff with your fingers and hands employs the large shoulder and torso muscles.

CLEAN YOUR SUNGLASSES with your weaker hand. Do your fingers tire? This can tire a shoulder, too. Prove it to yourself.

RINSE YOUR CAR or water plants with your left thumb over the hose end, forcing a spray pattern. How quickly does your fist cramp? Is your thumb burning? The arm and shoulder?

MIX PANCAKE BATTER with the weak hand. Use a big spoon. Let the right show the left how it's done (or vice versa), then tire the weak one and do it again.

DRUM YOUR FINGERS on a tabletop. How's the syncopation? Is it even? Rap both hands like you're playing the bongos. Do they feel the same? Can you articulate rhythms with either hand, or does the dominant hand still direct the emphasis?

Drummers-in-training do *rudiments.* To learn a beat, go only as fast as you can, as you work each finger fully through its requested range of motion.

Patterned training is slow and deliberate, by design. Guide or direct a finger through the movement with your other hand, if necessary. When you do it again a day later, you'll do it better. Guaranteed.

* * *

BECOME INTRIGUED by the certainty of improving your game and let creative desire provide you more exercises suited specifically to your needs. Count on it, and follow your instincts.

LIFE IS FULL OF PHYSICAL MOTION.

Most actions take surprising strength and dexterity to accomplish smoothly without

LEFT HAND IN THE GOLF SWING

thought, and are attended to with the stronger hand *out of habit.*

Consciously choose to use your non-dominant hand when you're able – when time permits or you don't have to do something perfectly or safely. Be careful using knives and power tools.

It may be laborious and time consuming at first, but *what better way to improve your golf than in the everyday living of your life?*

LIFE AS GOLF PRACTICE

If you love to practice, you've got it made.

YOU'VE GOT YEARS into developing the dominant hand, but it won't take that long to bring the weaker appendage up to speed.

Deploy the left and test it for yourself. Be patient. You're investing. Various tasks are accomplished over time as strength and coordination develop.

Progress with the left hand must be allowed to proceed pretty much at its own pace. More isn't always better, and 10 minutes a day every-other-day is sufficient. Muscles retain and remember the work when rested. Rest is training, too.

HIT BALLS OR PLAY FOR SCORE to measure your gains. If you're onboard, decide you're in it for the long haul. And so, persist.

YOUR GOAL in this is to produce lower average scores - thus a lower handicap - by **developing new physical talent that allows you to hit predictable shots - when and where you want to.**

Your game improves via awareness of new choices for any given shot, but ALWAYS with your bread-and-butter shot first.

Confidence grows when shot decisions are made quickly, then well executed.

Coming to Believe

We usually think professional athletes are *Naturals* - People born with a genetic grace that allows them to quickly perfect the athletic fundamentals of any sport.

We picture them fluid and perfect, free from the physical struggle and emotional turmoil inherent in our striving lives.

But it's not necessarily so, and there are drawbacks to being born a Natural. A young natural athlete with great footwork and rock-solid hand-eye coordination *doesn't have a clue* what it takes to develop what he possesses.

But take a Rocky-like character trained by a man who tethers his feet and puts him in a chicken coop to capture his lunch, and you've got an athlete who knows first-hand the effort and rewards of training his heart out.

That knowledge allows him or her to *fix things* that go wrong, and improve on things done right.

Much of the desire to excel is God-given, and athletes have a good deposit of it. Here's **George Will**, from his book *Men at Work: The Craft of Baseball:*

"Only a fortunate few have the gifts necessary to become great athletes. However, no *gift* is sufficient for greatness. Greatness is never given. It must be wrested by athletes from the fleeting days of their physical primes. What nature gives, nurture must refine, hone and tune. We speak of such people as *driven*. It would be better to say they are *pulled*, because what moves them is in front of them. A great athlete has an image graven on his or her imagination, a picture of an approach to perfection."

AN INJURED ATHLETE seeking to recover is put in a similar place of learning. Many times the effort, blended with a sincere desire to recover, will yield a better athlete – A smarter athlete with an appreciation of their gift as well as a better understanding of what it takes to repair or better it.

OFTEN IN ATHLETIC REHAB, talent is acquired or re-discovered, and ability regained or advanced IF there's the burning desire to work through the paces. An injury overcome makes a smart athlete a better one.

Desire to excel embraces those who embrace *it*. Make a beginning. The process becomes its own reward. When you hunger for change, you'll find your game.

* * *

I've an indelible memory of Bo Jackson - a football star turned Pro baseball player - In a game televised. He was immensely talented, though playing ball hurt in the early 1990's.

I remember Bo rounding third base, hob - logging for home on a leg with a dry hip socket. He had a heart like a locomotive.

Developing the off hand is truly about *that kind* of human effort. Make it a volitional act of the will, rooted in determination and an abiding faith in God, that **He provides the increase as you make the effort.** I believe you will not be disappointed.

GREG NORMAN, who has lived Pro golf's peaks of achievement and valleys of disappointment, gave this Wisdom as he added color commentary to a final-day tournament telecast:

"He'll have to rely on his own beliefs now, if he's going to bring this one home. They're what got him here. It's up to him."

The Nature of Talent

Ted Williams, the acknowledged greatest baseball hitter who ever lived, was deemed by sports writers to be a *Natural* with his smooth, fluid swing.

But Williams refutes it, referring to the *thousands* of hours he practiced his swing as a youngster, taking his stance and making cuts before a mirror; and playing sandlot ball most days until dark.

Good as he was, Williams never batted right-handed in a major league baseball game. Two-sided excellence is a tough act to perfect. It takes years for the wrists to comfortably break opposite to what they're accustomed, and for the spine and torso to generate power like off the natural side.

Only a handful of major leaguers end a season with a batting average over .300 off both sides of the plate, and only five have achieved it for a lifetime average, as of this writing.

The Atlanta Braves Chipper Jones, who first batted as a Righty, later taught himself to hit off the left side and is now more comfortable there. His averages prove it.

Ted Williams said he practiced THOUSANDS of hours to develop his swing fundamentals. He performed an hour of daily practice before a mirror - Taking his stance, seeing the imaginary ball in his mind's eye, swinging, following through and then retaking his stance again and again, until he finally got it right... until he could trust it under game pressure.

A thousand hours one-hour-per-day extends practice through the eighth month of the third year. Extending that standard to *thousands*, Ted William's natural swing would be better described as *self-made*. By his own admission.

Golf's Talent – Spawned by Left-Hand Strength

As beginning and developing golfers, we're in the dark about many aspects of our games. We listen, read and practice 'til our hands bleed, but we never really *get it*.

Improved ability is an awareness of broader opportunity in a specific shot choice.

When improvement becomes tangible, practice becomes a directed focus and the game becomes gratifying. It gives back.

TALENT IS ITS OWN REWARD

TYPICALLY, we've compensated and *overcompensated* our swings in various ways to keep the ball on line to a target. We lack the confidence to really *know* what the ball is going to do coming off the club face. (Perhaps not be you, now, but it was *me*, once).

INABILITY CREATES OVER-EFFORT

Compensating poor swing mechanics with a quick-fix or useless adjustment often brings the golfer to the point of critically analyzing the relevance of the sport in their recreational lives.

Why live frustrated, we ask? We're jammed up, tired and tired *of* it. *Stymied,* in golf lingo.

We've jostled with stance and ball position. Tweaked the grip. Moved closer to the ball. Moved *away* from the ball. Gotten technical with our swing plane or pronation vs supination with no clue what THAT means.

We hear the talk and talk the talk, but we can't walk the walk.

* * *

DILIGENCE AND DESIRE for elusive self-knowledge pays dividends to those with the fortitude to hang in and go after it.

Moments of clarity stand out – recalled as a defining moment when it all made sense and success was at hand. One pure shot can do that. And so we remain golfers, because *Golf Keeps Calling*.

TRUE TALENT is rooted deeper - in proper fundamentals. Confidence is born when your method is working. There is no feeling in sport like ripping a ball with an athletic golf swing.

TALENT OFFERS NO APOLOGY

The Formula is developed and coordinated power in the left hand and left side of the body.

YOU'VE GOT A CHOICE: Either strengthen the weakness or accept the shortcomings you've compensated for all your life.

Coordinate your strength and your perspective will change. Try new things different ways and you'll start having more fun out there. Coordinated strength is *key*.

Talent developed this way sneaks up on you. It just arrives, with no memory of the effort it took to acquire it.

STRENGTH NEVER OVER TRIES

ONE DAY ON THE RANGE, you'll realize you've got something new going on in your swing. Solid contact takes less effort. You're aware of it but don't have to think about it or consciously exert undue force.

You can all-of-a-sudden do something new with the club; it just *feels better* in your hands, or your turn seems simpler and more concise. You're working an effortless draw; off and running through an enjoyable bucket of balls.

* * *

YOU MAY BE considering these exercises and applications a revelation ... information that's new to golf. Just invented. Your self-talk may be saying, "Yeah, but…"

Perhaps you seriously doubt the validity? Nobody blames you. There's a lot of golf information out there. *Everyone's* got a plan to get you swinging the club effectively.

But this is not new golf stuff. The

presentation is varied, but these are the *fundamentals,* drilled down and described in detail.

Fundamentals Need No Defense

If it's relevant information that speaks to your golfing mind, why not run with it? Creative thinking and innovation is everywhere – in life and sport.

Club makers and equipment marketers constantly present N*ew-and-Improved* to the marketplace. Longer, Softer, Bigger, Better with More Spin and more carry ....

Technology has advanced golf, no doubt; And if you feel various equipment makes you play better – Buy It. But to score better, you've still got to swing the club and make square and solid ball contact.

GOLF IS A GAME THAT HAS TO BE PLAYED

A philosopher named **Herbert Spencer** wrote some notable words on disbelief. He said this:

"There is a principle which is a bar against all information, which is proof against all arguments and which cannot fail to keep a man in everlasting ignorance – that principle is contempt prior to investigation."

Dominant vs Subordinate Theory

In his classic book *The Ambidextrous Universe*, Martin Gardner writes on bilateral symmetry, which is left/right dominance in the feet, eyes, ears and even the chewing of human beings. Bilateral symmetry is fundamental to the bodies of animals. Survival of the species hinges on its effective use.

Humans, birds, animals and most species of fish have left and right eyes, fins, hands, feet, hooves, paws, ears, noses, etc... developed for use by the up-and-down effects of gravity and the forward-and-backward directions of locomotion.

We're focusing on developing your left/right effectiveness to enhance your golf and recreational life, but don't sell yourself short.

PRESIDENT JAMES GARFIELD had a remarkable personal talent: He could write in two classical languages at once. According to a 1998 article in the National Review by Tracy Lee Simmons:

"James Garfield took his early education at a modest school in Ohio, where he drank heady draughts of Homer, Herodotus, Livy, Tacitus and Virgil. It was said that, years later, the ambidextrous Garfield could hear a sentence and translate it on paper, one hand writing in Greek, the other in Latin."

BABIES ARE BORN ambidextrously uncoordinated, but a child can't stay klutzy for long. There are too many ways to get hurt in the playpen.

Children learn this at an early age, so one of the hands takes control in the tricky manipulative endeavors - things like turning over the cereal bowl or seizing a toy from a sibling. The most effective hand gets the call. Kids are Rightys or Leftys in their first five years.

THE DOMINANT hand becomes the controller in the golf swing. If one is ambidextrously coordinated – even handed – S/he naturally produces a more balanced swing.

THE BODY of the ambidextrous athlete develops and delivers power smoothly through a wider swing arc, moving the hands in sync with the coiling and uncoiling body and more naturally applying weight shift to the swing in balanced harmony.

Photography reveals that a golf club *pulled*

through the ball with the left hand strikes the cover a bit more *flush* - without a cupping action the film makes apparent when the blow is delivered with a push from a dominant right hand.

* * *

Ben Hogan, Arnold Palmer, Johnny Miller and Tom Watson rank high among left-handed golfing greats who played right-handed.

Bobby Jones - perhaps the most intellectually articulate golfer besides the mature Ben Hogan - was right-handed and believed *that hand's responsibility* **was to provide power to the hit at the bottom of the swing.**

Jones minimized speaking of the left because strength there was natural to him. He had enough self-awareness (of his left) to re-grip the club at the top of his backswing. Watch his tapes. It was a personal idiosyncrasy that reveals *everything* about his left-side strength and control.

Jones said the left's biggest responsibility was that it pulled well, and that the elbow didn't break down in preparation for the delivery of the clubhead. That alone requires developed strength.

* * *

Ben Hogan has described in detail his seeking balance at the bottom of the swing to counteract the coiled power he delivered with his natural left side... from his legs, torso and shoulders, down his arm and through his natural left hand.

MR. HOGAN likened the feeling in the hands at the bottom of the full swing to throwing a medicine ball with the right. The left hand controls the club, the right hand delivers the power, and the swing is initiated from the legs up.

TEACHING PRO HARVEY PENICK likened the release of power at the bottom of the arc to the feel of swinging a water-filled bucket.

THESE DESCRIPTIONS are more than *semantics*. This is how two of the best players and teachers in the game conveyed their *true beliefs* about the golf swing. It is a description a golfer knows only by feel.

Patterned Training

Patterned training breaks down the mechanics of a sport to its elements, allowing analysis of form and function - The individual working of certain parts of a whole.

Sports like water skiing are taught on dry land – Patterned Trained. Students walk through the physical motions they want their bodies to do over water, at speed.

The student holds the ski rope handle, stands in the skis (or ski) and leans alternately left then right against the pull of the secured rope. The body learns the feel of the mechanics prior to entering the water. It must be taught, but the body remembers, and aspires to exceed your expectations.

IT IS GOOD TRAINING to pause the golf swing and observe the parts of it - to feel what you're doing. PGA Professionals teach by this technique.

Swing a golf club with one hand; first your left, then your right. Grasp the club where your hand would normally be on the grip. Stop, get quiet, close your eyes and do it in your mind's eye. Which is the more palpable memory?

Most players say the mental feel is not as vivid in their non-dominant hand.

* * *

TYING THE MENTAL to the physical is one of the best ways to gauge and improve personal athletic ability.

One can perform an athletic endeavor only as well as one can mentally do it, and one can do better physically the *mental endeavors* one does best. This is visualizing, applied.

As learning takes hold, expect improvement in the *feel* of the activities you're practicing. Both mental and physical.

All players feel the clubhead in the waggle (much of the waggle's purpose, and to bleed tension).

Some players say they can't feel their hands gripping the club at the top of the backswing, yet swing for the feeling of ball contact as their hands deliver the clubhead at the bottom of the swing.

Golfers encounter mental blocks at certain swing stages that are unique player-to-player.

Talent connects the mental flow of the feeling to the physical application. You earn this through persistence. Don't quit. Just keep showing up, and always expect a breakthrough. As stated, you sometimes have to own all of a thing to become aware of it.

GOLF GETS BETTER when you can mentally hit the shots you want to hit before you hit them. Keep practicing.

DO THE 10-SWINGS-A-DAY DRILL through thick grass, for excellent feedback. Not tall grass, but clumpy grass that adds resistance to the club face coming through it.

Reverse your grip to practice 10 swings off

your unnatural side. If you're Righty, swing Lefty, and vice versa.

It'll feel weird at first, but you may discover as the fingers get comfortable in the reverse swing, they're even MORE comfortable holding the club in their natural grip.

We may be covering old ground here, but golfers do it all the time on their home course. Nothing succeeds like success. Practice it.

Cross-Training is Transference for Power & Control

Athletes seeking to know the subtle intricacies of an unfamiliar sport can develop essential skills through cross-training a similar sport in which they have better ability.

Sometimes success is the result of doing something else or something different. Cross-training and drills are all about that. Effort here can be profitable.

Though practicing a new and unfamiliar activity (like golf) will no doubt create a level of proficiency in it, cross training the muscles to do a different-but-similar physical motion enhances ability beyond simply practicing the new or unfamiliar one.

Cross-training educates the muscles necessary to allow you to sidle up to a more difficult activity and bleed the talent into your developing sport.

Things begin to feel more right to you as you internalize the nuances of the new sport you're learning. You've jumpstarted the learning process by practicing the sport you know well.

SPEED, EFFICIENCY and PROFICIENCY most succinctly define ability here. I like the term *Fluid Hydraulics* to convey the power, grace and pleasure of excelling in a physical activity.

ABILITY IN THE UNFAMILIAR activity increases as the variables brought to it from knowledge of the Familiar sport take root and become an improving part of it.

Often, immediate feedback is available to apply to the familiar activity with an exactness the self-aware enthusiast recognizes as notable improvement. This includes hand/eye coordination, activities with the hand, arm, shoulders and torso preparation, and to mobile dexterity.

* * *

TENNIS and FRISBEE are two popular sports/activities that emulate the pulling

LEFT HAND IN THE GOLF SWING

action contributed by the top hand in the golf grip. Left hand for Righty golfers, right hand for Leftys. Cross-train these.

For Righty's, the Lefty tennis backhand and the Lefty Frisbee toss sew power and touch into the developing left hand, arm shoulder and torso. Just mirror with the left what the right does with it if it's sub-par. Pattern-train in front of a mirror, if it simplifies things.

If Lefty tennis is totally new to you, pattern train with *air swings.* Just do the physical rudiments. Practice the high backhand volley and notice how the empty hand wants to extend out some and scissor across your chest beneath the racket to counter balance the pulling motion of each backhand air volley. Let this happen. Your body is learning.

Add a ball and a wall, and you get a lot of stroke practice in a short period of time. Get to know the wall if you cross-train with a racket sport. It will pay dividends. Hitting against a wall is easier than playing an opponent, because the pace of the ball's return is predictable.

Let the ball bounce. Swing easy. Just keep it in play to develop your sense of timing and touch. Power and control come with ability – via practice.

Volleying without the ball bouncing is the next step. Keep it in the air against the wall. Playing it back to an opponent on a court adds another element.

Dribble the ball with the forehand and backhand sides of the racket. The backhand dribble trains the strength needed to control a supinated wrist. It will also enhance control of the Lefty backhand volley, which is excellent golf cross-training. And mentally, it all relates back to golf.

A LEFTY FRISBEE workout in the cart barn when it's raining can be a worthy group lesson. Boomerang the Frisbee into the wind, if you've go no one to send it back.

TENNIS, RACQUETBALL, FRISBEE, hockey and baseball offer great cross-training benefits.

Soccer builds footwork and leg strength that provides stability in the swing. Basketball develops footwork as well as athleticism, taking the mind off the work of it.

Shooting and handling a basketball with the non-dominant hand builds wrist and arm strength, and will let you get a fix on just *how much* of the weak side torso is called upon when used in different sports.

What does all this have to do with the golf swing? Plenty.

DYNAMIC ATHLETICISM BOOSTS POWER & STABILITY THROUGH THE ROOTED STANCE OF THE GOLF SWING

The more functional the legs are in a dynamic sport like surfing, skateboarding or skiing, for examples, the more stable they are when planted in spikes beside a golf ball. And the better they channel power up through the clubhead into the back of the ball.

MIX ANY OF THE ABOVE with some of the off-hand use in your daily living and you've got a full plate of athletic endeavor to contend with.

Because talent evolves, you'll gravitate to more difficult cross-training activities that further tune your ability, or you'll just get better at the ones you're doing, bringing better ability to your golf.

The mechanics of both will become more *articulate,* because you're bringing ability from the new sport back to the sport you're better at. The mechanics work more fluidly or with more speed, thereby enhancing precision.

THE TERRAIN in cross-training changes as talent expands – As you are transformed.

New choices and knowledge of enhanced ability is the feedback of self-awareness the athlete processes to determine a further course of improvement.

Stoking Your Passion

Most athletes are turned off by the Rah Rah - *Watch the Ball and Keep Your Head Down* coaching of their formative years.

One gains athletic endurance by finding the Heart in the endeavor... the Passion. Passion heightens intrigue after token interest is worn away.

Mature athletes reason calmly with their competitive selves. They don't waste emotion on self-chastisement. They forgive themselves quickly, evaluate the takeaway – the lesson learned – and move on.

Forgiveness comes first. You can't think straight with a head full of anger – negative passion.

TED WILLIAMS said the hitters he hung with in his early baseball years were out there after practice with him banging balls until dark. Men in their 40's... in the twilight of their careers, who couldn't get enough of hitting the ball. They had a passion for it.

VINCE LOMBARDI, revered former Green Bay Packers football coach, on Passion:

"Every time a football player goes out to ply his trade, he's got to play from the ground up – from the soles of his feet right up to his head," the Great Coach exhorted. "Every inch of him has to play. Some gutsy play with their heads. That's OK. You've got to be smart to be No.1 in any business. But more important, you've got to play with your heart – with every fiber of your body."

DON JUAN, protagonist of author Carlos Castenada:

"I travel the paths with heart or any path that may have heart. And the only worthwhile challenge is to traverse its full length... so there I travel. Searching, searching breathlessly."

AFFIRMATIONS are statements like the above by those who've been there. They're worth reading. If you read something that inspires you, commit it to memory, then lean on it. It will pay dividends.

TEDDY ROOSEVELT, on Competition:

"It is not the critic who counts... The credit belongs to the man who is actually in the arena... who strives valiantly, who errs and comes short again and again... who at best knows the triumph of high achievement and who, at worst, fails while daring greatly, so that his place shall never be with those cold and timid souls who knew neither victory nor defeat."

GREAT ATHLETES ARE STRONG ON THE INSIDE

GET YOURSELF INSPIRED, break down your goals to manageable pieces and address them one day at a time. Do the details. 10 swings a day is a detail. So is 10 minutes of concentrated effort. The journey of a thousand miles begins with the first step. Getting in the game is the main thing. No time like the present to make a decision.

Wisdom of a Hall of Famer

In his 2002 Hall of Fame induction speech, former St. Louis Cardinals shortstop Ozzie Smith shared the following wisdom:

"Ozzie Smith was a boy who decided to look within, a boy who discovered that absolutely nothing is good enough if it can be made better...a boy who discovered an old-fashioned formula that would take him beyond the rainbow, beyond even his wildest dreams."

Then Ozzie shared the formula. Comparing his life to Dorothy's journey down the Yellow Brick Road in the *Wizard of Oz*, Ozzie said the secret is to develop *the Mind to Dream* that the Scarecrow cherished, *a Heart to Believe* that the Tin Man ached for, and the *C-C-C-Courage of the Lion* to *Persevere.*

"I used to throw a baseball over the roof of the house, then try to run around and catch it," Smith said. "No, I never caught it, but it never stopped me from trying. Luckily, I didn't just experience the dream for a moment and then dismiss it as foolishness."

SUCCESS TAKES ENDURANCE

Never doubt it. It takes a game plan. There will be forks in the road. Many choices and lots of decisions. It pays to know your own talent – to *know what you know and what you need.* Get that and you're on your way to seeing your progress and accepting the process.

Don Juan, on Commitment:

"A man goes to knowledge as he goes to war: Wide awake, with fear, with respect, but with absolute assurance. Going to knowledge or going to war in any other manner is a mistake, and the man who makes it will live to regret his steps."

Being Convinced

The intent is to teach you to coordinate your non-dominant hand, to balance your golf swing and to let you have more fun out there.

Golf improvement is a process. If you've made a decision, schedule time to work at it, then climb aboard. Age doesn't fit into this equation. You *can* teach an old dog new tricks, if the dog is willing.

How Important Is It To Focus On The Subtle Specifics?

Well, how well do you play with a splinter in your toe?

To the extent something as small as a splinter affects your overall well-being, so does development of various and smaller muscle groups influence your ability to perform a certain physical dynamic.

Touch is born in the small muscles, with movements stabilized by the large muscle groups off both sides of the body. The uncoordinated muscles must coordinate for any athletic endeavor to be performed with finesse or fluid power.

Expect frustration. There will be times you'd prefer dynamite to a shovel to level the mountain. You're fine-tuning things. It's *your* golf swing, so make it your own. Patience is key here, but ENDURANCE is the better word for it.

The difference between luck and skill is style. Style is personal to your innate ability, and it is uncovered as much as created. You're beginning a process to make your golf swing your own. To know it and own it.

It's been your destination, getting to here, to Start This Process. So what if it took all the physical effort and mental gyrations golf put you through to get you here, to this understanding - To this Beginning? It's what got you here.

Is there an end to it? Does one ever *Arrive?* Nope. That's the short answer. Few golfers are good enough to quit.

Bobby Jones retired from competition at age 28, but everyone else through golf's history capable of wielding a club probably worked on their golf games all their lives - And enjoyed it.

Ted Williams on the Work Ethic

In his Hall of Fame acceptance speech delivered July 25, 1966, Ted Williams said:

"...ball players are not born great. They're not born hitters or pitchers or managers, and luck isn't the big factor. No one has come up with a substitute for hard work....I've never met a great player who didn't have to work harder to play ball than anything else he ever did. To me, it was the greatest fun I ever had, which probably explains why today I feel both humility and pride, because God let me play the game and learn to be good at it."

WORK HARD. It doesn't take much to tire you with drills. Do it regularly. Be patient, and deal with the inherent weaknesses uncovered as you experiment.

I found it difficult to simply lift the extended ring finger of my left hand, with the fingers flat on a table top. I anguished over it, and could only attempt it several times at a sitting. The disgust in my spirit was similar to when I rattle a 3-Iron off bad contact. Not a good form of recreation.

IMPROVEMENT IN THE SPORTING LIFE may not be so difficult for you. Progress is personal. No one walks in another's shoes, and nobody knows what's inside you. You won't either, until you challenge yourself.

TALENT DEVELOPS as strength in your weaker hand develops. It works on a gradual, upward spiral: New strength being the forbearer to ability, and increasing ability creating incentive to find new ways to develop strength.

THE SIMPLE TASKS we do every day take surprising strength and dexterity to accomplish gracefully, but they CAN be mastered. Practice them in your mind. Conjure up your best recollection of a drill, then put it away.

As you are challenged to balance manipulative strengths, solutions will naturally come up and your intuitive mind will begin to present you with more. When stuck, do the drill right-handed and copy the action to the left.

CONSIDER: You'd be ambidextrous had you used your weaker hand to do whatever you now have a dominant hand performing. So now you're on your way with it, making conscious choices.

Reference - Five Lessons: The Modern Fundamentals of Golf

In his classic instructional, "Five Lessons: The Modern Fundamentals of Golf," Ben Hogan described essentials of a sound, powerful and repeating golf swing. An *athletic* golf swing.

One fundamental is the golfer be

supinating the left wrist before impact (for the Righty). Supinating is the rolling over of a relaxed wrist that leads the clubhead through the back of the ball.

The opposite of supinating is pronating. It is *cupping* the wrist through the bottom of the swing. That makes for bad golf. Grab a baseball bat and take your batting stance with it. You've most likely pronoted both wrists – locked them out, to be solid in handling the bat.

TO CLARIFY PRONATION & SUPINATION – EXTEND BOTH HANDS, fingers out. Rotate the thumbs downward. You are Pronating those hands. Raise the thumbs. You are Supinating your hands.

ASSUME YOUR GRIP with the left hand at the butt of the club. Take your stance with the club on the ground before you and move your hands as a unit, opening and closing the club face.

Pronating (or cupping) the left hand supinates the right hand, and opens the club face. Pronating the right hand supinates the left hand and closes the club face.

Now set the club at the top of your backswing and work your hands.

Consciously pronate the left hand. The right hand supinates and the club face is opened. The toe of the club shifts (points) away from the target, behind you. Look back at the toe to verify this.

Consciously supinate the left hand at the top of your backswing. The right hand pronates as the left supinates. The club face closes. Note the club face shifts (points) *toward* the target – the green or whatever is on your target line.

Delivering swings utilizing aspects of supination and pronation will shape shots – work the ball right or left in a fade or draw.

MENTALLY WORK these concepts through to an understanding and convince yourself the golf club is an implement that can be controlled. The above is just *some of the language* used to describe how to control it.

Trial-and-Error proves pronation is the stronger physical motion, and more sustainable. Use of a screwdriver or turning a tough doorknob with the extended hand will reinforce this.

IT IS AN UNNATURAL ACT FOR A DOMINANT RIGHT-HANDED GOLFER PLAYING WITH RIGHT-HANDED CLUBS TO SUPINATE THE LEFT HAND AT THE TOP OF THE BACKSWING AND RETAIN CONTROL OF THE SHOT.

The weaker left hand seeks the strength of the hammer grip, which locks the wrist out when pronated for strength. This opens the clubface. You'll be lucky to hit a power fade from here. More than likely, you'll get a steep slice.

IDEALLY, THE STRENGTHENED LEFT HAND LEADS THE DOWNSWING & BALANCES THE POWER OF THE DOMINANT RIGHT

THE SUPINATED LEFT HAND must possess strength to be the controlling force in the downsing. The right hand works in silent unison with the left – delivering power into the ball at the bottom of the swing, but not before. And the dominant right must stay passive at the top of the backswing, to keep the club on plane. That's often difficult for a dominant right hand to do.

STRENGTH IN THE LEFT IS THE ANSWER

IDEALLY, THE CLUB is delivered to the back of the ball from inside the line with the club head squared and closing – with the left hand supinating.

The strong left hand that supinates through the bottom of the swing develops some very desirable actions. It creates a wide and sweeping forward arc in swinging the club, and it allows the player to fully extend just after impact, utilizing all the expendable clubhead speed that has been stored in the backswing, Hogan said.

Crisp contact made to the back of the ball

is evidenced by shallow, scalloped divots that begin in front of the ball, not behind it.

SUPINATION IS UNNATURAL BECAUSE IT IS WEAK. BUT IT CAN BE STRENGTHENED THROUGH DRILLS & ACTIVITIES

IN THE OPTIMUM GOLF SWING, the dominant left hand is leading. Hogan describes a pulling motion with the left; not a push with the right.

"At impact," said Hogan, "the back of the left hand faces toward your target. The wrist bone is definitely raised. It points to the target and, at the moment the ball is contacted, it is out in front, nearer to the target than any other part of the hand".

Stiff and rigid and locked out doesn't work. Pronated doesn't facilitate a fluid golf swing for shots out of the fairway or off the tee. It feels good – strong – But it works against the golf swing.

You may pronate, cup and lock out the left wrist for a steep swing at a cut shot out of a bunker or deep grass, but that's about it. That and the high pitch, or *flop shot.*

THE SUPINATED LEFT HAND must possess the strength to be the controlling force in the downswing of the clubhead.

THE BEST WAY TO HARNESS THE DOMINANT RIGHT HAND'S CONTRIBUTION IS TO DEVELOP A LEFT ARM AND HAND

THAT - WHEN SUPINATED - IS STRONGER THAN THE PRONATED RIGHT.

"Every good golfer has his left wrist in this supinating position at impact," Hogan said. "Every poor golfer does the exact reverse."

When a golfer's left wrist begins to pronate just before impact, it changes his arc," Hogan said. "It shortens it drastically and makes the pitch of his upswing altogether too steep and constricted".

I'VE BEEN GUILTY OF THAT.

"By changing his arc and plane," continued Hogan, "the player frequently catches the ball too low on the blade and skulls it, or hits the back of the ball. If the face of the club is open, he gets a big scoop slice."

I'VE BEEN GUILTY OF THAT, TOO.

THE CONCEPT of pulling the clubhead through the back of the ball with the left will keep your body behind the ball better than any swing thought out there, because it's not a swing thought. It is pure and proper mechanics.

* * *

PGA TOUR PRO Phil Mickelson is a well-publicized example of a golfer using his dominant hand to pull the club through the swing.

Phil's a Righty playing left-handed, brought up that way in the game by an astute father who understands the simple dynamic that's it's better to PULL an implement through a defined space than to PUSH it.

Phil's dad was rightly convinced the coordination in the pulling chest, shoulder and arm muscles are more exacting and precise in their delivery of power through a clubhead that follows a strong leading arm.

* * *

Because it's joined at the grip – Because it *Can* - The dominant right hand of the right-handed golfer takes control of the golf swing.

When the left hand supinates – AS IT SHOULD – the right naturally pronates along with it, *activating its strength*. That's a strength that must be delayed until power is released at the bottom of the swing.

STRENGTH IN THE LEFT HAND OFFSETS OVERRIDING POWER IN THE DOMINANT RIGHT.

Ben Hogan understood the golf swing's difficulty when he said, "Reverse every natural instinct, and do the opposite of what you're inclined to do, and you will probably come pretty close to having a perfect golf swing."

Handball – The Ambidextrous Sport

Handball, boxing and swimming perhaps are the only true, two-handed sports - But even boxers fight regular or southpaw. Ambidextrous water polo players are sought after, since they can throw the ball with either hand.

In handball, the worthy competitor is only as good as his off hand. The weaker one. All else being equal - the player with the better weak appendage should work an advantage and win.

Handball players develop elaborate strategies to compensate their weaknesses.

One style, called the *Sword and Shield Strategy*, describes the sword as the strong hand – usually the right – and used primarily for offense. The shield is the defensive appendage - typically the weaker left hand.

When competing, the strong hand hits the ball with offensive direction and power while the weak hand just keeps the ball in play.

Handball champions are ambidextrous athletes with equal power in both hands. Their advantage is twofold: They can offensively return any shot hit them, and they don't have to think about NOT being able to hit a particular shot.

Consequently, strategic thinking comes to the forefront because two-handed ability is a given and the player is not shielding a weakness.

DOES THIS SOUND LIKE GOLF TALK, AS WELL? OF COURSE IT IS..!!

HOW MANY SWING FLAWS ARE ROOTED IN INABILITY..?? WELL, THAT *IS* THE GAME, ISN'T IT?

GOLF IS ALL ABOUT ABILITY, OR GETTING AROUND 18 HOLES WITH WHAT YOU'VE GOT.

Few of us Amateurs can hit *all* the shots with *all* the clubs, but golfers who hit through the broadest range of shots most proficiently shoot the lower average scores.

FOR YEARS I PLAYED GOLF FOR *FUN*, but couldn't hit the long irons. I lunged at 'em. I was a fighter out there, but that isn't golf, and the game had me frustrated, because baseball had ingrained many bad habits.

We savvy contact hitters tend to cut across the ball from outside-in, gripping the bat with the hands locked out and rigid.

Pronated. That's good hitting, but it's not a good golf swing.

THE BASEBALL SWING is good for rhythm and warm up, but hitting a baseball doesn't do much good for the golf swing because it doesn't train any articulate range of motion when taught from baseball's point-of-view.

If you drill with a baseball bat, use your golf grip, and swing it like a golf club in front of your toes with your feet close together. The bat has weight, and is a good strength trainer.

* * *

I REMEMBER WATCHING Tour Pro Davis Love at the World Golf Championships at Lake Nona in Orlando a while ago. That was the first time I'd seen a great player up close doing subtle things with his hands. There are subtleties TV just doesn't pick up in the telecast.

On one memorable shot, Davis took the emphasis off a wedge at the point of contact, and just *feathered* the ball to a tight pin from about 100 yards.

He didn't decelerate on it; he just hit it with an awful lot of touch. It was a clinic on how great players manipulate the clubhead into the ball. Their feel for the ball is *phenomenal.*

GOLFERS who cannot hit a particular shot weigh their options and calculate the odds of making any particular shot – to advance the ball safely toward the hole. They weigh the risks against the rewards before executing the shot.

This is good course management, but if you can't hit a full complement of golf shots, you're setting yourself up to add strokes in lieu of better scoring that talent will induce.

CONSIDER: Few players can hit a driver off bare ground, but back off that extreme, look at other tough shots and you'll get my point. If we can't get the *distance* we need, we lay up and pass over the chance, say, at an Eagle putt on a particular Par 5.

If we don't trust our swing on a hole loaded with water, we may hit away from it, adding strokes to our score.

Writing Lefty – A Worthy Endeavor

Writing may be the single most beneficial exercise one can do to develop the off hand.

It immediately puts numerous muscles to work.

Writing is a powerful isometric exercise – because movement of the pen or pencil point is minute and exact. There is minimal contraction of muscle fibers. Instead, the muscles are working in concert to hold fast the pen to paper in a functional mode.

It is more of a bearing down, and phenomenal tension training for control. Muscle tone, strength and dynamic articulation are enhanced from the fingers to the shoulder.

Begin by pattern-training the mechanics, however slowly you have to go about it. Write the 26 letters of the alphabet. Then form the capital letters. Form the letters with the left like when you learned cursive writing in 3rd grade.

It is likely to be tedious, perhaps agonizing work. Persist and form the letters, however tough it is. When your hand cramps, rest it, then form them again. Do this every day for even just a few minutes, and you'll get results.

TRY WRITING YOUR NAME left handed. Write the capital letters. Scribe the numbers. There are only 10. Spell them out. Write them as words. Gauge your progress against your recovery time, and don't worry about the quality of the writing. It will improve.

Give yourself time in this, and note your improvement when you come back to it. The muscles of the hands are supple – not bulky – and strength is acquired slowly, so the fingers remain nimble. That's how they're wired.

Keep a scratch pad handy and make notes left-handed as you listen to your phone messages or brew coffee in the morning. Practice while your computer boots up. You may not even doodle well in the beginning. Nobody did.

What a Novelist Said About It

In The Ambidextrous Universe, Martin Gardner relates a tale from Vladimir Nabokov's novel titled *Look at the Harlequins!* in which the narrator suffers from a peculiar pathology that is his lifelong torment: He cannot, in his mind, imagine how to turn himself around so that left becomes right.

The mental parallel of visualizing the left hand in the golf swing is too useful to ignore. **Nabokov writes:**

"In actual, physical life I can turn as

simply and swiftly as anyone. But mentally, with my eyes closed and my body immobile, I am unable to switch from one direction to the other. **Some swivel cell in my brain does not work** (boldface added). I can cheat, of course, by setting aside the mental snapshot of one vista and leisurely selecting the opposite view from my walk back to my starting point. But if I do not cheat, some kind of atrocious obstacle, which would drive me mad if I persevered, prevents me from imagining the twist which transforms one direction into another, directly opposite."

THAT SWIVEL CELL in the brain works only as well as one's best-recollected memory of the experience. It can be maddening - The awareness of the mind's inability to sequence spatial memory in an acceptable connectedness - with Synchronicity.

CAN YOU FEEL THE CLUB AT THE TOP OF YOUR BACKSWING..??

The best physical memory of any technique is usually culled most completely from the last experience of its attempt. The memory can be most clear after a few days rest, prior to another training session, but before the work of it.

Your awareness of the clubhead in the backswing will improve as comfort, strength and dexterity of the non-dominant hand is worked, and then rested.

Said philosopher **Ernest Holmes**:

"... man (a male or female athlete) has not yet evolved to a complete understanding of himself. He is unfolding from a Limitless Potential **but can bring into his experience only that which he can conceive** (boldface added). We can demonstrate at our ability to know. As a man's understanding unfolds, his possibilities of attainment will increase."

BE VIGILANT IN SURVEYING the shifting landscape of your athletic improvement in honest self-assessment. Expect results in increments over time, and acknowledge your improvement – however subtle.

If knowledge is power, the power is gained by taking a different look at the same problem and figuring out new ways to solve it. Call it a paradigm shift, if corporate terminology suits you.

Try Mirror Writing

One of the difficulties in writing with the off hand lies in pushing – not pulling – the pen across the page. It's not what you're accustomed to.

Try writing in both directions... pulling the pen from right side to left with the left hand (if it's the left you're developing). Form the letters in reverse. Sounds weird, but that's the way Hebrew is read and written and it's a more natural motion for the left hand.

We're accustomed to writing thumb-to-pinky with the right in a relaxed, flowing style. Pulling the pen right-to-left across the page mirrors the same action in the left hand, and it's exactly the way the left hand wants to articulate the golf club through the ball.

IT DIRECTLY REPLICTES THE SUPINATION AND RELAXED LEFT HAND HOGAN DESCRIBED AS ESSENTIAL TO THE FLUIDLY FUNCTIONAL GOLF SWING

Reverse writing with the left brings a lot of useful golfing muscles into play. Practice it. You'll feel your arm working up into your shoulder. If it's burning, muscles are working.

You'll eventually be able to write well in both directions. When you finally get it going on - Developing the feel of it - Reposition your elbow and see how it affects the way you form your letters. Most likely you'll set up a whole 'nother challenge for yourself.

THE NATURE OF PROGRESS IS A PROCESS

Over time, writing long sentences will become second nature to you. The talent and strength of it will be incorporated into your upper body.

Write standing up, and you'll be able to tell from the tiring muscles through the arm and shoulders just how much of your body you've got in use. When you think you've arrived, try writing with a dull pencil into a thick sheaf of papers. That's an acid test.

Work of the Thumb

The hands would be no more than claws without their opposing thumbs.

YOUR DEVELOPING OFF HAND will be only as strong as its opposing thumb in ability to clutch the grip and deliver power.

You'll note quite a variance in relative strength between the fingers, wrist and thumb.

Don't discount the thumb's influence in the golf swing, just because it's wrapped up in overlapping fingers and braced by the heel of a hand. It supports the club shaft at the top of the swing, but that may be its easiest job.

The thumb is a pivot point and provides manipulative leverage in the swing. It adds power to the leading hand - The hand gripping the butt of the club, and it influences the rate and pace of the wrist break as it rolls over when coming through at the bottom of the swing.

It takes five fingers to effectively hold the butt of the club, so work hard to make your left thumb independently strong. You've got 10 fingers and two thumbs. Go figure. Get 'em all strong.

* * *

Repetition rotating your left thumb with the same authority as your right will develop latent strength and dexterity in it. Can you pop either of them? Roll your thumb in its socket right now. A thumb that 'pops' has more dexterity and strength.

SIT IN A CHAIR and allow your extended thumb to support your offside hand and arm from a pivot point just behind your kneecap or on top of your thigh.

Use your thumb strength to rotate your hand in a circular motion, then side-to-side and back-and-forth. You'll get a quick read of your thumb's innate strength, as well as strengthen it.

THE THUMB or the pinkie finger might be the last appendage to develop focused coordination. Don't let a slow rate of progress discourage you. Progress is progress.

HANDLE THE WEIGHT of that open dictionary or big Bible again in your outstretched left hand. Half the weight or more is over the thumb, depending where you opened it.

Get a burn goin'. Open it and snap it shut, then change the page angle so you can read from it. This is a great strength builder for your fingers and thumb, hand, arm, shoulder and torso.

SEEK PROGRESS, NOT PERFECTION.

YOUR STRONG HAND has been serving you ably all your life. NOW is the time to bring the off hand up to speed. The left WILL respond to the challenge you throw its way.

The body is *amazingly adaptable* when you push it then rest it. Just pay attention to what you're doing, and be persistent. Be patient but persistent.

BUTTON OR UNDO a button with your non-dominant hand. Observe how the fingers tweezer the small stuff. The thumb plays a big part in this *tweezering*.

Use the dominant hand then try the other one, turning the intricate endeavors around. Remember how it feels.

The dominant hand *knows.* Slow it down and let it teach your off hand everyday, mundane tasks. Repeat the process daily, and take note of your progress.

Speak To Your Muscles

You've been discovering an absence of muscle tone and dexterity in your off hand – which is 90 percent of any population's left. It can be discouraging, but stay positive.

Your uncoordinated left has been doing the best it can with its golfing assignment since the day you began handling a golf club.

Expect new recognition of ability as the left hand develops. Begin its development by determining your weakest points and chart a course of improvement. How? If holding the dictionary tired your left hand quickly, make a point to look up words regularly, holding that big book in your left. Be disciplined.

If your front door key tweaks your shoulder or hurts your thumb when you turn it in a dry lock left handed, persist anyway, and consciously use the left.

FORM NEW HABITS

Sounds simple, but you won't want to at first. Deploying the left is strange to the way your body normally works. It is new physical work. Experts say it takes about 19 days of repetition to break a habit, or form a new one.

BE STEADY AND REGULAR with your activity schedule. Specific training to any determined athletic deficiency will lead to identifiable improvement over time.

Big muscles develop more quickly than little ones. The muscles of the wrist and forearm are slim and supple, and develop more slowly.

As stated, if they weren't supple, they'd bulk up and dexterity would suffer. We're not wired that way, so that won't happen, but consequently, gains in strength with dexterous activities take time and repetition.

But you're used to repetition from hitting range balls. Remember? You've just changed your game up a bit.

It may take weeks to develop enough strength to grip the club a certain way with the left hand...To where it FEELS different in your grip.

The different feel correspondingly sends new signals to the brain about how the club *now* feels at the top of the swing, which then may allow a longer pause at the top, or a more deliberate move into the downswing.

WHEN IMPROVEMENT PROVIDES ITS OWN REWARD, PRACTICE BECOMES FOCUSED AND THE PROCESS BECOME SATISFYING

Expect new awareness (talent) to be substantive and visceral.

What you see and feel in your mind's eye becomes more readily transported to the physical realm, and improvement in the physical realm reinforces and improves the mental memory of it.

THIS IS HOW the golf game improves... slowly, vis-a-vis your expanding awareness of potential and choice with any given shot - But ALWAYS with a bread-and-butter shot first, or a certain club. Maybe a 7-Iron, or perhaps your Gap Wedge.

Improved ability provides the opportunity. Gauge your progress against a shot that's been your personal nemesis.

Know Thyself

Knowledge of my shortcomings settled in my spirit as a profound understanding. *I simply became aware of how bad I was with my left, and the work necessary to improve it.*

ACCEPTANCE FOSTERED COURAGE to self-assess my unmanageable set of golf swing problems. I'd tried golfing around them for years, but had always had a clear understanding of just where I stood. I couldn't hit the long irons, and I was stuck.

I took action, knowing I had all the time it would take to learn some new physical mechanics. I played college tennis as a Righty, so I had no left hand strength, to speak of.

I worked a plan 10 minutes a day every other day, with my tennis racket in my left hand, for a change. I tell it as *my process* to building balance into my swing. Your story will be your own - Similar but Different.

THE EFFORT AND COMMITMENT demanded in thoroughly training the weaker hand keeps most golf instructors mute on the subject. Tell your PGA or LPGA Professional, coach or golf teacher what you're doing, if you use one.

Most likely they'll support you and show you some drills they save for students in it for the long haul. There's nothing as honest as desire. If you're hungry for improvement, get going. Let progress feed your passion.

TRUST YOURSELF AND TRUST THE PROCESS. You've got what it takes – we're hardwired for improvement - and you don't need anyone to tell you much of anything else.

Self motivate. Listen to the Whisperings, and work your plan.

Facing Your Fear

WHETHER FEAR WAS EVER REAL to the greats in their sporting games is unknown to me. It is their belief system, their story to tell and their business to tell it.

Some Pro athletes are born with huge talent. Others develop it day-by-day, like the rest of us. Their reckonings with it are in their stories. All have dealt with a Dark Night of the Soul in facing early athletic challenges, or contemplating retirement. It is humbling when your best is not good enough.

* * *

Time dulls memory of fear that beset me before I accepted knowledge of my athletic shortcomings. But it was real to me then.

Fear sat heavy in my gut - Like a bowling ball - Quietly disputing all the practice I'd ever put into the mechanics of my golf swing - Trashing all the confidence my work ethic had deposited there.

A DECISION TO CHALLENGE YOURSELF can be one of life's scariest moments and most rewarding determinations, at the same time. Resolve trumps fear. Self-belief moves mountains. If you seek progress rather than perfection, you can begin that walk at any moment in life.

IN GOLF AND LIFE, the journey IS the destination. If you believe ONE MAN can make a difference or ONE BOLD ACT or DECISION, then you're at a point of departure.

It could be where you've been headed all along in the Divine Plan for your Golf Life.

BEGIN YOUR JOURNEY

Embracing the desire to grow your game is an ongoing process of change - Of physical growth accompanied by the mental understanding of it.

You are transformed. Your *nature* changes. There is new comprehension and confidence. Each talent shift adds tint and hue to the path of progress. It lends flavor to a shifting landscape, like the newness of travel on a cross-country trip.

Or, to bring it back to golf, in the gradually strengthening hand that adds finesse to your short game and variation to your shot selection. Change brings confidence, not uncertainty.

* * *

AVID GOLFERS OF *ANY AGE* are young enough to BE ENTHUSED about having a go at a bucket of range balls after work. Look forward to it. Relish your plans.

We play games for fun, so enjoy your preparations. Anticipation is the well-spring of desire. So are Hope, and Improvement and Success. Expect all these in this endeavour.

AS YOU COLLECT THE REWARDS of progress, sidestep regret for paths taken that lacked heart... yielded scant reward or wasted your time and money.

The world is full of trickery and quick fixes. It took every treacherous step of the journey to get you where you are today - r*eady to begin that new walk in knowledge...to humble yourself to the rudiments of learning.* Count the costs and face them every day. Or don't count them and just face what comes.

THE JOURNEY IS AS MUCH A PROCESS OF UNLEARNING AS LEARNING SOMETHING NEW

THOUGH WE LIVE in a world of statistical knowledge that binds judgment to intuition, I still like Han Solo's declaration in Star Wars: *Never tell me the odds*. That's belief. An overload of data can thwart the decision to commit. Procrastination sows deep and devious roots.

MOUNTAINS DISAPPEAR AS TALENT PROGRESSES

Sure it takes time to impart certain abilities into your body's coordination, but once acquired, the blood and sweat is lost in the exhilaration of the bettered performance.

On the other side, finally, you may wonder why acquiring new talent *seemed* so difficult at the time. You may recall diminished memory of that effort as the will applies itself fresh every day to the new task at hand.

IF THE MIND DIDN'T PERFORM THIS MENTAL CLEANSING, YOUR PASSION WOULD DIE & YOU'D BURN OUT

Instead, with every Sunrise, the mind and body awaken and immediately begin using renewed ability to tackle the tasks of the day and perpetuate further gains.

In *Golf Is Not a Game of Perfect,* author Dr. Bob Rotella said professional athletes are challenged to think in the most effective and efficient ways possible.

He calls it the *Psychology of Excellence,* explaining the concept of *free will* allows the experienced golfers to let thoughts control events rather than have events control their thoughts.

Choices have consequence. Golfers who readily forgive themselves bad shots swing from a level playing field.

"They create their own realities," Rotella said. "The Pros develop a short-term memory for failure and a long-term memory for success."

Sounds like the right way to be thinking.

* * *

TALENT ACQUIRED is a transfiguration of your body's knowledge. Rate of progress will vary, so appreciate what comes as your muscles integrate themselves to the effort.

Talent is most appreciated as it proves the truth of its benefit. It *will justify* the work it took to get there. All we as athletes do and seek and aspire to in this physical realm is to improve.

We cannot become worse diligently seeking to improve the fundamentals. We can only become better, and first, always, in our minds.

WHEN JOHN DALY WON the Buick Invitational after eight winless years on the PGA Tour, he credited fellow Pro Peter Jacobsen with telling him something that strengthened his resolve.

Jacobsen said, *"No matter what happens, John, the talent never goes away."*

"That stuck with me for a long time," Daly said.

RE-LIVING YOUR PLEASURABLE GOLF MEMORIES reinforces the thinking you had when you created them. The pleasant memory of a good swing will tend to make that swing yours, and a part of your game.

Negative thinking, on the other hand, is almost 100 percent effective,

... SO DON'T DO IT..!!

INSTEAD, use your selective memory and imprint the good memories into your brain, and forgive yourself the bad ones.

Create Your Own Reality as Dr. Rotella suggested. Golfers must let thoughts control events rather than have the outcome of events control their thoughts.

"This goal is to get your mind where it's supposed to be on every shot. If you do that, you'll shoot the best score you're capable of shooting that day, whether it's 67 or 107," Rotella said.

* * *

IT IS NECESSARY to practice the things you don't do well, to improve.

Why is a 3-Iron harder to hit than a wedge? Is it the flatter swing...the longer reach to the ball? Does the wedge's shorter length get the clubhead through its hitches before it can waver off line?

The reasons are many – all correct – and all unique to you, the player.

GOOD GOLF is spiritually nourishing to watch and remember.

Most golfers will agree there's not a much lovelier sight in golf than a player standing calmly over a long-iron shot, executing a seemingly lazy takeaway that works into a full backswing that suddenly but unhurriedly flourishes into a downswing that delivers the clubhead flush into the ball, with a full-turn follow through that relaxes back off the torque...the soul-resounding *thwack* delivered so crisply into our living rooms by the TV mike it becomes the sound we seek in our contact.

Develop Your Own Program

Set reasonable goals, and work a schedule. Do the details. Diligence here is somewhat about the work ethic, but if you miss a few days, just pick up where you stopped. Rest is training, too, so don't beat yourself up. Make it fun, and stay away long enough to get hungry again, if you get fed-up.

It takes time to get results. Don't compromise. The rewards are BIG when your work bears witness in your golf swing.

Your game develops a life of its own. Golf becomes fun to play and practice.

THERE'S A CATCH-22 in the development process: As ability increases, so do the choices in the way you can swing the club. So the better you get, the tougher it is. Not tougher by design; tougher by the choices that will tempt you to go for more, or go for broke.

There are cut shots, the draw, flat swings and fades and all points in between. Greater choice in how to work the ball creates greater responsibility to do so well, and to stick to a winning game plan, because there is more room for error. Avoid the ego-driven self-sabotage of dismissing risk vs reward evaluations or expecting more than you know you can deliver.

Golf's a hard game. It's physical *and* mental. If it were any other way, they wouldn't call it golf. Spell *GOLF* backwards for a better understanding. Aha aha.

Doing & Being: Work & Rest in the Learning Process

Consider visualization as the *Being* part of the equation. It is recollecting what is already known. The ability to visualize one's knowledge of the golf swing or a particular aspect of it is based upon one's best memory of the experience.

The *Doing* is the physical, real-life side of the equation. If Doing enhances one's ability in an endeavor, it also enhances the memory of it. So the *Being* gets better. Talent arrives.

ONE CAN RELATE the learning curve's awareness of Doing & Being to the steady better view of a landscape observed by walking up a stacked deck of playing cards spun in a helix.

The very subtle change in the view as one climbs the card stairs is similar in ability and perspective gained through the Doing & Being process.

Recall the best visual memory of what you *know you can do* – *Being* – with the practice of physically moving the body through the *new mechanics* of *Doing* the particular activity. Expect to do it more efficiently in the future, and have a better mental memory of it, as well.

And always you rest – allowing the muscle's tissue to internalize the work.

DO & BE = WORK & REST

Whatever you're attempting becomes more Efficient, through Practice, over Time. Practice makes perfect more quickly than playing does. Playing sets the benchmark, when you're serious about improvement.

LOVE TO PRACTICE and you'll always play well, if you focus on the ailing elements of your game. All golfers are working on *Something*. The goal is to lower the benchmark – play better golf. Shoot lower scores.

Practice the hard things, and do them in your mind, too. To overcome a mental block, *cut & paste* your best memory of the endeavor to the effort of doing it with the other hand. Meld it.

Making the mental process fluid is the work of it. It is tiring. Accept that, but *attempt it* daily, if even if only for the few seconds you may be able to stand it. Just pay attention to it without grimace or angst.

DEXTERITY IS SPECIFIC TO THE ACTIVITY

ONLY THE DOING of a particular activity improves your body's precision in the activity. Cross training assists, but you've still got to do the activity you're trying to improve. Do both. Alternate.

One player could volley a tennis ball, but couldn't dribble it with the racket until THAT PARTICULAR EXERCISE was practiced with the off hand. That's the way it works.

There are subtle areas and elements to develop. Ability in something new will reveal a weakness in its variants. Make notes as you contemplate your progress.

* * *

WORK ON bouncing a tennis ball lightly on the forehand and backhand sides of the racket strings while sitting quietly or watching TV.

Just handle the racket. Keep it in your hand and hit air volleys – without the ball, if it happened to have rolled across the room.

Do the same with your putter or wedge, if you want to get comfortable with a club. Get it in your hands when you're at rest, and get comfortable with the feel of it.

DON'T BE SURPRISED BY WHAT YOU LEARN AS YOU CHALLENGE YOURSELF

WATER FOLLOWS THE PATH OF LEAST RESISTANCE, and so do we humans, many times.

You're working against the grain of all your habitual thinking here, but you're gaining an ability to think, feel and act in a more comprehensive manner – A two-handed manner. Both sides of your brain are firing information to both sides of your body.

OWN THIS PROCESS and incorporate the drills into your physical living. You are well on your way to becoming a better athlete, both in the ways you move and in the ways you think about moving.

Though cross-training and practice are essential to make you better, only Doing a particular activity will prove the body's precision in it, so play golf for score to establish those benchmarks. Always keep swinging the clubs.

Train Then Trust

All athletes must rely on their instincts to deliver a great performance. Golfers, bowlers, tennis players and javelin throwers...they do the rudiments until the rudiments are innate, then they simply focus on their targets.

Limited ability in the physical mechanics necessary to capably manipulate a golf club results in high-handicap golf. Cross-training certain elements of the swing while continuing to swing the club is the formula for growing your game.

You'll do some of these activities easily. Others may take real work before you begin to obtain some proficiency in them. Do the easy ones and try hard on the tough ones so you can figure things out. Set the easy ones aside as you master them, and keep working your plan.

THE GOOD NEWS IS you *can* and *will* improve. You *can develop* a repeating, athletic golf swing. 10 minutes a day every-other-day is sufficient practice to grow your game. Every day isn't too much, if you're thirsty.

Expect to start each day renewed and focused on a better base of ability. You're on the path to being even-handed. There's no time like the present to seek a balance of power.

Pain as a Price for Progress

When you challenge your body into new routines, it'll fight you some days. Expect that.

Nobody knows your tolerance for pain, frustration or aggravation. Not even you, until you face it. Time is a healer. One must trust the body's ability to adapt when pushing it to new and uncharted athletic levels.

IT ISN'T PAIN UNTIL IT HURTS

One player described a lot of shoulder pain as she learned to serve the tennis ball left handed. She'd broken her left collarbone playing softball in her twenties, and felt she was into a difficult undertaking teaching this seldom-used appendage to do something *Totally New*.

Swimming helped, she said. She rehabbed it using various strokes, and then the tennis motion came easier. Getting the weight of her shoulders out over the handlebars of a 10-Speed helped her build sustainable strength.

ANOTHER PLAYER DESCRIBED PAIN in the tips of his fingers as he rolled them across the outside mirror of his pickup.

It was painful – bad as a steel splinter – and he realized the cartilage in the finger tips of his seldom used left hand was never broken down and made supple like his right. He worked through this one in a couple of days, accepting the pain for the gain.

STEADY PAIN in the palm of my developing left hand lasted about 30 days. The throbbing would awaken me nights. It baffled me, because I'd been slapping a handball with it for a couple of decades.

Didn't matter. New is new, and I was using it differently. I numbed it with ice cubes for a while, reasoning the tendons, cartilage and blood vessels were adjusting to work new ways in the hand as I learned to work the hand in new ways. Then it went away.

PAIN WILL HIT YOU IN THE FACE

IT IS BETTER TO DECIDE NOW not to quit when pain pays a visit. Stay with your game plan. Every boxer has a strategy until he gets hit in the face - a given in that sport. Victories are won by the action taken afterward.

Athletes are used to a certain level of pain in their lives, and experience an acceptable level of it during and after every workout. They live with it.

Serious athletes who seek to lower times or increase speed or lift more weight push themselves hard within a common and familiar realm, working within a threshold - and then beyond it - by design. They're exhausted, but bettered by it.

Do the same with your off hand. Work it hard, then rest it. Be patient, but persistent. Allow time for physical recovery. Muscles will ache and joints will cry out for relief. Give them that, but be persistent. Be diligent.

NEVER WORK PAST A PHYSICAL CATCHING POINT WITH ANY KIND OF VIOLENT ACTION

When seeking results, press to a point of tolerable pain, hold it, and then back off.

Injuring yourself creates no shortcuts. Press on, but stay patient. If the rudiments are difficult, do them slowly in patterned-training mode.

Any constraint or hitch encountered in an athletic endeavor can be overcome by meeting it head on, or by cross-training with another activity that strengthens the muscles necessary to allow you to sidle up next to it and figure out what it's going to take to get you doing it the way that works best for you.

Both strategies are effective - and *most effective* when used alternately.

SPEED and EFFICIENCY and POWER are three variables that most succinctly define success of a strategy.

Never change a winning game, but if your progress is stymied, try something new. Be diligent in all your endeavors, applying steady effort over time.

Give it 110 percent, to the point of exhaustion. Rest, then do it again. And again. It takes that kind of work to instill new mechanics into athletic motion.

REST IS TRAINING, TOO

The boxer Oscar De La Hoya said the above, when asked by the Press why he was relaxing poolside the day before a fight. Believe in it.

PUSH HARD to extend your limits. Only your own effort will tell you what you're capable of. All good athletes push the envelope to know their strengths and weaknesses. Tested ability is better trusted.

Smart players play to their strengths. As strengths broaden, opportunity abounds in new shot choices and real added distance.

* * *

YEARS AGO a construction foreman told a griping worker: "Everybody has a bad back." The longer I live, the more I realize this may be true.

Witness Fred Couples dealing with his back at The Wachovia Championship one year in Charlotte, N.C. Fred never complained, though it buckled his knees. Great athletes rarely do, publicly. They save it to direct the trainers and health care professionals.

YOU'RE EMBARKING ON a challenge a bit more difficult than obstacles encountered by the typical weekend warrior.

Becoming an ambidextrous athlete is a commitment, and making the off-hand mechanics second-nature is Work.

You'll be pushing your limits. Pain and frustration are on your horizon, but remember: You are the sole judge of your standards. View pain as weakness leaving the body, and decide now what you want and what you'll settle for.

PAIN IS WEAKNESS LEAVING THE BODY

Dr. BOB ROTELLA: "Though I teach psychology, I have never known for sure where the mind ends and where heart, soul, courage and the human spirit begin."

"But I do know that it is somewhere in this nexus of mind and spirit, which we call *free will*, that all great champions find the strength to dream their destinies and to honor their commitments to excellence," Rotella said. "All great champions are strong on the inside."

Fluid Power Has No Constraints

Gaining strength through your hands and fingers will lend you power in the application of an event – Plus it will allow you to fully stretch and relax in the preparation of the application.

One cannot coil tensely in preparation to pound a big drive or feather a chip.

Ernie Els – The Big Easy - hooded a 5-Iron back in his stance from beneath a tree at the 18th hole of The Doral Championship some years ago.

Crowded by – almost hemmed in - By respectful spectators, Ernie was peaceful. He had a crease in his slacks, and one in his shirt sleeves. No strain on his face as he set up over the ball.

Big slow draw of the bow and powerful, fluid contact. No strain, no grimace at the hit. He punched it with a three-quarter swing, hitting a low shot that snuck under the tree branches then rose into a slow climbing draw that found the green on the fly, bit then rolled out of site over a little hump this side of the pin. Focused but at ease, Ernie let go the trace of a smile as he observed the good result.

* * *

FEW MEN IN GOLF handle the clubs with the kind of deliberation as does Fred Couples, a Lefty who swings from the right side. Couples has been quoted he'd just as soon take his right hand off the grip when hitting delicate sand shots, but hesitates doing so to avoid the appearance of showing off. He wouldn't be. Talent is not ego.

Fred's statement is chock full of talent *and* humility, but I'm not speaking of his short game here. Fred Couples uncorks crushing, deliberate power with the finesse *of* the Short game.

Witnessing his focus, I'm reminded of Ben Hogan's absorbed reply when asked by Ben Crenshaw how he keeps a 5-Iron beneath the wind: "I try," said Hogan, "to hit it on the second groove."

WHEN COUPLES started putting left-hand under, I was still witnessing convincing Pro incidents that edified the left-hand theory of golf's fundamentals.

I was privileged to witness his second shot at the Par 5, 13th Hole at Augusta National on Sunday, the final day of the 1998 Master's Championship, the year Mark O'Meara won. Fred toasted an iron to within a few feet of the pin. He really rocked it.

"Oh Baby," he said, quoting Barry White. Yeah, it was that good, and Fred *couldn't have said more.* He had entered into golf's *Holy of Holy's* with that swing.

Rock solid in balance and heart, the swing was just the demonstration of his consciousness. The short putt the result and the reward.

The Incredible Efficiency of Unweighting

A turn on a surfboard or skateboard is made with a push or pull with the front foot, augmented by the counter-balancing torque of the other foot at the tail of the board.

It takes strong and coordinated legs to make power shifts in footwork on a surfboard, or in snow skis or on dry land. The key is unweighting oneself prior to moving the feet.

Unweighting with a quick directional step can torque the upper body to instant preparation for forward, lateral or a rotating dynamic action.

A SIMPLE SIDESTEP can load power. The legs move from just below the waist - from the trunk down. The entire leg moving to a pre-set position can also wind the torso, and load a preparatory movement of the shoulder, arm, elbow or hand.

The common phrase *Power is rooted in the legs* is all about this level of footwork. It requires a toe bounce with a follow-up quick repositioning of the legs to a *pre-driving* state.

PERHAPS THE BEST EXAMPLE is what

Muhammad Ali could do with his *Ali Shuffle.* No one had seen it before Ali, and no one has done it well since. The quick footwork was the source of his preparation, allowing him to deliver lethal power in a short punch. Effortful work, yet Ali did it with dazzle. It was the root of his style.

LEGS HAVE DOMINANT and non-dominant aspects, too. A lady who surfs Goofy Foot – right foot forward – Drives and controls the surfboard with her back foot – her left one. You'd think it would be the stronger leg, through constant use, but *it's not.* She says she balances better on her right leg in the one-legged yoga postures. Go figure – and consider carefully.

PLAYING BASKETBALL, you may think you're stepping *forward* with your front foot, but you're really *driving off the back one.*

Though the legs are larger muscles and burn more calories in motion, unweighting gets the knowledgeable athlete around the fatigue of it.

THE GOLFER UNWEIGHTS, as well. The front foot may lift at the height of the backswing at full torque, then set and receive the full body weight in the torque of the follow through, as the trailing leg lifts to allow it. The parallels are real. Some feet lift more than others. That's an element of style.

* * *

ONE OF THE BETTER GOLF ARTICLES through the years used infrared photography to portray how rhythm and power are distributed by the legs.

The sequence of photographs changed color (red-to-yellow-to-blue) to distinguish the different pressures exerted by each foot through the various stages of the golf swing, measured by a pressure-sensitive mat.

The flow of colors was a visual display of rhythm coordinated to the club's position in the swing, from setup to follow through. It revealed all the subtle and drastic variations in downward force, as the feet supported the body through to the swing's completion.

Talent, Ability & Heart

AN ATHLETE can be ambidextrous at some things but not in others. Seek balance in the physically easier things first.

The adage **you can't get there from here** really does apply. Certain muscles and muscle groups must be developed before others are *smart enough* to do their thing. Putting the cart before the horse just leads to frustration.

THE TIMELINE FOR PROGRESS WILL BE YOUR OWN

Let the strong arm model whatever you want the weaker one to learn. Train then trust. Groove it in your mind, then teach it to your body.

Though it may appear linear, a circular motion in the mechanics of preparation and delivery is common to all sport. Ability in the tough stuff will line up and fall into place as strength coordinates. There's really no other way to go about it.

Don't be afraid to break it down to the rudimentary details. You'll learn more about what your natural motion is doing as you pay close attention to it.

THE CHALLENGE IS TO REVERSE THE THINKING AND APPLY IT TO THE WEAKER SIDE

Prove to your innermost self you *can* improve, and then devise your own schedule.

Make it fun, and don't beat yourself up if you get overwhelmed or frustrated as your dead reckoning comprehends what you're undertaking here.

If you miss a day, skip the next day, too, or more, 'till you get hungry again. 10 minutes a day every-other-day will yield identifiable results sooner than later.

Re-Thinking Right Thinking

The Lefty vs Righty phenomenon has intrigued other great athletes.

While TV commentating a US Open Tennis Championships some years ago, John McEnroe marveled how difficult it is to play tennis with the off hand (his right).

Johnny Mac had the consummate left hand in tennis. He put his whole body behind the stroke and just COVERED the ball.

He'll have some work to do to train his right side to deliver similar power, but if he stays intrigued and works at it a bit every day, ability will make its way to him. And Mac's got the best teacher in the game in his left hand.

IT IS ASTONISHING THE HARDEST SHOT IN TENNIS IS EQUAL TO THE ROUTINE GOLF SWING.

And you wondered why other Pro athletes respect golfers..?? Because they *know*.

As stated, the left hand tennis backhand IS the golf swing. Actually it's a blend of the high backhand volley off the left side and the backhand ground stroke.

That's the golf swing, and the high backhand volley is the last bit of ability most tennis players get. You've got to have the whole game to get the high backhand volley.

And the backhand overhead is a notch above that – one of the tougher athletic endeavors in sport. The shot demands powerfully supinated strength in the wrist.

IT TAKES REAL STRENGTH TO LAY A WRIST BACK WITH CONTROL

The supinated left wrist laid back and delayed or held to volley a backhand down the line closely emulates what Ben Hogan described as the ideal wrist position when coming though the ball at the bottom of the golf swing. That is what you're working toward.

Two-Sided Cuts with a Baseball Bat

Swinging a baseball bat is a great way to develop athletic rhythm and to loosen up before golf.

Learn to swing from both sides of the plate, and reverse your hands.

It's a good drill for getting familiar with your body's weight shift, and it strengthens your wrists and hands - though what the hands accomplish in it do very little for your golf swing unless you use your golf grip.

USE BOTH – the baseball grip *and* the golf grip - realizing the difference in terms of pronation and supination (pg 26).

Set aside fear that one will negatively influence the other. Both strengthen the wrists. They are separate but similar. Practice to gain understanding of both dynamics.

As in golf, the hips initiate the swing and lead the torso around ahead of the bat. Swing hard with your feet set at golfer's width, *but don't stride toward the mound like a hitter.*

Instead, finish with your hips cleared and your leading leg locked and bowed toward the target, just like the ideal golf finish.

The drive and follow through on either side extends and stretches the shoulders much to where they operate in golf, and makes profitable demands on the arms. It's good to get the lower back used to torquing both ways, as well.

The way the hands finish holding the bat in the left-handed follow through exemplifies the control the same left arm needs in the backswing of the right-handed golf swing, and vice versa. Strive to swing smoothly off both sides.

ASSUME YOUR GOLF STANCE with the bat, using your golf grip. Handle it like a wedge. The extra weight of the bat's barrel will weigh heavier on the hands at the top of the swing, and when you swing through. Make slow swings to build strength.

THIS IS CROSS-TRAINING AT ITS BEST

REMEMBER: Forget the stride when working with the bat. Not striding more nearly simulates the balance your legs do with the golf club. It takes a narrower stance to do this fluidly.

Weak legs seek a wider stance, but rhythm flows better through a narrowed one. The hips clear quicker. Strong legs can be stable in a narrowed stance.

The awareness of the feet distributing their balance of power as the clubhead works through the ball IS rhythm. Power in the legs augments it.

Dynamic power is necessary – the kind gained from doing squats, done with or without weight across the shoulders.

Certain static yoga postures that demand one-legged balance are excellent strength trainers, as well. As well as soccer, basketball, basketball, skateboarding and everything else suggested.

The Fluid Hydraulics

ONE OF THE BEST METAPHORS for physically impacting a golf ball is the visual image of a door slamming. Ever really watch that happen?

Picture the wind grabbing an open door. It starts it moving almost imperceptibly and accelerates gracefully until it slams shut with a velocity that will rock a wall.

THE GOOD MOVE into the golf swing is similar. It is stationary at some point at the top, when you reverse the club's direction.

Then it becomes an accelerating, powerful blow that is an accumulation of linked forces, powerfully delivered into the back of the golf ball.

Harry Hopman, the great Australian tennis coach, said nothing so encourages the spirit as the *soul-satisfying 'thwack'* of a well-hit tennis ball.

That aptly describes the power of the great American tennis champion, Don Budge, who had one of the best backhands in tennis. True because his string application at contact was so deliberate and well directed. Solid.

GOLFERS who strike the ball well hit it *flush*. No sport so much as golf affords so little margin of error in getting that soul-resounding flush feedback from good contact.

Balls well hit nourish the soul, slaking a thirst you never knew you had. You'll crave perfection but be satisfied with your best, knowing when you've got it and when you got above it.

* * *

NOW GOLF STARTS GIVING BACK, and all your work takes meaning.

EFFORT IS RECONCILED BY SUCCESS.

There's a frame around your experience, and you wouldn't trade the investment. Sweet redemption. Your mind finds and defines pillars of excellence – The notable successes that inspired your cross-trained committment; where you hunkered down and finished a job, and you start to understand Ozzie Smith and what he meant by **Nothing is acceptable that can be made better.**

An interest in the Rules of Golf defines integrity in new and acceptable ways and whets your appetite for the knowledge and wisdom of it. And you learn. Every day there's a takeaway.

* * *

IF YOU WATCH much golf on TV, you'll

begin to identify golfers from a distance by their swings. There are idiosyncrasies to the manner in which a golfer sets their hands at the top or brings the club through. Or turns their body. Or takes their stance.

The difference between luck and skill is style, and style is predicated on ability. Habit develops style around efficient application of the fundamentals.

THE MAIN BENEFIT of the strongly-developed left is the enhanced awareness and *feel* of the club in the swing.

Increasing knowledge allows the golfer to get the club face started down on the desired line (from inside, with the face closing) and with the foreknowledge s/he is doing it in an efficient and effective manner.

The suggestions discussed have sought to convince you the key to this is the articulate, controlled strength of the hand that handles the butt of the club.

A Word of Caution

Be careful to not let your strong arm atrophy. Keep it in shape as you develop the weaker one.

One player completely quit using his right for a while as the left improved, even doing Nautilus with only the left, because the right had so much innate natural talent, it made the work done on the left seem useless after a workout, he said. The right's talent overshadowed everything, so he let the right slide.

MUSCLES ATROPHIED, and were strained in a tennis match that couldn't be won with the developing left hand.
Core strength left idle lacked muscle tone around some elbow tendons. The injury healed, but it took a while, and re-strengthening the right became a process much like developing the left.

The moral? Keep your whole body in shape, even while you focus on a specific muscle group.

The Subtleties of Strength and the Elements of Power

Good athletes give it just what it needs. They swing within themselves - within the limits of their control.

How often do you hit the ball harder than necessary? It's easy, isn't it, to get pumped up and drive a ball over a green or past a safe landing area or through a dogleg?

Good golfers never rush the swing, yet they're never late. Gaining strength through the hand and fingers will not only afford you the necessary power in the application of the mechanics of an event, but it allows you to fully stretch and relax in the preparation of the application.

One cannot coil tensely in preparation of an athletic technique. You've got to relax to throw a baseball or hit a tennis serve or drive a golf ball. Though always explosive, the hit is delivered from a relaxed state of preparation.

Touch requires strength. Touch and feel and finesse without strength is tentative, too careful and often jerky. Inconsistent, at best.

Most big men who are athletes (read: Coordinated) have extraordinary touch. Raymond Floyd was known for it. Former Tour Pro John Daly's source of touch around the green is born in his controlled power.

NOTHING IS SO STRONG AS GENTLENESS, NOTHING SO GENTLE AS REAL STRENGTH – Native American proverb

John Daly's philosophy off the tee is to just *Grip It and Rip It*, and he's been the PGA Tour's longest driver.

But Daly wouldn't tout that saying if he didn't have extraordinary control of the club head. John Daly is one of the best athletes in golf.

Always Do Your Best

Swinging within yourself is one of the hardest aspects of any sporting endeavor. So is giving it your all without over-cooking it.

Astute golf teachers tell children to hit it hard while learning, knowing they can settle back into a level of control as their ability matures. That's good advice for any student.

Practice working back and forth, from maximum effort to 80 percent of it, with control. That said, whatever you're trying to accomplish with a club, always give it 100 percent of your attention and intent, in play or practice.

Jack Nicklaus has said that because we're creatures of habit, habitually failing to keep trying when it doesn't matter conditions a part of ourselves to accept the lesser effort, making it harder to call up our best effort when it matters most.

Coming to Know the Athletic Golf Swing

Golf is a state-of-mind that becomes a way of life. Your maturing, balanced power creates opportunity to work the ball and the responsibility to do so well.

There is more room for error, and your analytical mind will find ways to challenge your ability to the point of self-sabotage. So keep the ego in check, and keep it simple. The object is to put the ball in the hole. No need to angle one off a tree trunk, even if you can.

Applied knowledge will make you your own best coach, enabling your athletic mind to see itself differently within the problem *and* the solution.

Talent gained never goes away. Keep it, it's yours. You've earned it. Use it to enhance your quality of life. So go to work now, if you believe, and develop your game.

References

Castenada, Carlos. The teachings of don juan: a yaqui way of knowledge (1968). New York. Simon and Schuster, Inc.

Gardiner, Martin (1972). The ambidextrous universe. New York. Charles Scribner's Sons

Hogan, Ben (1957). Five lessons: the modern fundamentals of golf. New York. Simon & Schuster, Inc.

Holmes, Ernest (1938). The science of mind. New York. Penguin Putnam, Inc.

Rotella, Bob (1995). Golf is not a game of perfect. New York. Simon & Schuster.

Smith, Ozzie. (2002, July 29). 'Wizard recalls storybook career.' The Daytona Beach News-Journal, p. 6B.

Will, George. (1990) Men at work: the craft of baseball. New York. MacMillan Publishing Co.

Williams, Ted. (1969). My turn at bat: the story of my life. New York. Fireside books

About the Author

R.D.HILL is a native Floridian whose passion for handball spawned a life interest in physical development. Hill golfed since childhood, but played poorly. "I couldn't hit the long irons," says Hill.

"I was convinced golf is a left-handed game played sideways by right-handed people." Hill was stymied until an interest in tennis left-handed developed new ability in golf.

Convinced '**As the left goes, so goes the golf game**,' Hill writes to simplify golf – a game in which subtle intricacy IS the draw, as well as the drawback.

"Sports like golf, with the difficult physical mechanics, *seem* like a mystery to those who've missed essential instruction, been led astray or listened through ears of disbelief," says Hill. "*Anyone* can learn to apply some routine athletic fundamentals into the rudiments of their swing and obtain real personal satisfaction from golf."

"Your whole body is the golf swing," says Hill. "Activities and Drills with your non-dominant hand – whether Lefty or Righty – will help *Balance* your swing as you apply all the elements of power to the back of the ball. It's a simple formula."

Golf's a great way to be outside. You deserve to get real personal satisfaction from The Greatest Game. Let *Left Hand in the Golf Swing* make it Fun for You..!!

Made in United States
Orlando, FL
23 November 2021